THE
HIGHLAND CLANS

BOOKS BY L. G. PINE

The Stuarts of Traquair
The House of Wavell
The Middle Sea
The Story of Heraldry
Trace Your Ancestors
The Golden Book of the Coronation
They Came with the Conqueror
The Story of the Peerage
Tales of the British Aristocracy
The House of Constantine
Teach Yourself Heraldry
The Twilight of Monarchy
A Guide to Titles
Princes of Wales
American Origins
Your Family Tree
Ramshackledom
Heirs of the Conqueror
Heraldry, Ancestry and Titles
The Story of Surnames
After Their Blood
Tradition and Custom in Modern Britain
The Genealogist's Encyclopedia
The Story of Titles
International Heraldry
Sons of the Conqueror
Acteon: History of Hunting in Britain
The New Extinct Peerage

THE
HIGHLAND
CLANS

by

L. G. PINE

BA LOND, FSA SCOT, FJI, FRAS, FRGS
Barrister-at-Law, Inner Temple

DAVID & CHARLES

NEWTON ABBOT

0 7153 5532 5

© 1972 L. G. Pine

First published 1972

Set in 11pt on 12pt Baskerville
and printed in Great Britain
by Latimer Trend & Co Ltd Plymouth
for David & Charles (Publishers) Limited
South Devon House · Newton Abbot · Devon

Contents

1   An End—and a Beginning

ON 4 DECEMBER 1745 an army which had marched from Edinburgh on 3 November reached Derby, only 125 miles from London. In the great civil war in the seventeenth century between the English Parliament and King Charles I, the Scots under good generals had marched as far as Preston, and even in 1651 to Worcester, though on the latter occasion the invading army had been by no means wholly Scottish. Both at Preston and at Worcester the invaders had been completely defeated by superior military intelligence and the genius of Cromwell. In 1745 the Scottish army did not represent the Scottish people, most of whom were opposed to it, though quiescent in its partial occupation of Scotland. It did not exceed 5,500 men, of whom 4,500 at least were clansmen from the Scottish Highlands, men speaking a foreign language, brought up and living under a semi-feudal system quite different from that prevailing in the rest of the British Isles.

The leader of the army was that figure of never-ending romance—Bonnie Prince Charlie—Prince Charles Edward, known in history as the Young Pretender and by a polite usage in English society as the Chevalier St George. He was the elder son of the Old Pretender, known to his adherents the Jacobites as James VIII of Scotland and James III of England; his grandfather, James VII of Scotland and James II of England, was the last male Stuart to reign in the three kingdoms, and was held by the English Parliament to have abdicated when he left England in 1688. He had been succeeded on the throne by his son-in-law, the Prince of Orange, who reigned jointly with James II's daughter as William III and Mary II; followed by James's younger daughter, Anne, then by the German princes, the Electors of Hanover, who through the distaff side were descended from the Stuart kings.

The male-line Stuarts in exile never gave up hope of regaining their thrones and the attempts they made will be described in due course, because they depended for any chance of success on the support of the Highland clans. Likewise the '45 Rising, and in order to understand the clan history and position, the events of the '45 must first be outlined. Several factors made the attempts of the Stuarts to regain their thrones much less foredoomed to failure than they now appear. Ireland was never for long easy under the English yoke and James II had found great support when he landed there in 1689. In the Scottish Highlands, the clans were a source of anxiety to the government in London, one reason being that they were the only people in the British Isles known to have weapons in their homes. It was also widely believed that there were many Jacobites in parts of England and Wales ready to rise for the Stuarts provided that sufficient support was forthcoming from France. Here was the weak point in the Stuart cause.

Louis XIV had welcomed James II to St Germain and allowed him to set up a court and to plot against the British Government; more than that, when James was dying, Louis had promised to look after the interests of his son (the Old Pretender). This was all very well when France and England were at war, which they were almost perennially from the reign of Queen Anne (1702–14) until Waterloo in 1815. France began to appear as the national enemy of England and the dynastic struggle of Plantagenet and Valois in the fourteenth century took on the aspects of a quarrel between Englishmen and Frenchmen. France did not, however, do much for the Stuarts beyond using them as an irritant against Britain; occasionally supplies of arms and military advisers were landed from France for the Jacobites, but the one step which could possibly have meant success for Jacobitism—the landing of a large French army in Britain—was never taken. It may never have been contemplated by the French, though they did use the threat as a means of tying down British troops in Britain, and the probable reason for their decision was the superiority of British sea power. Although it was not until 1805 that the Royal Navy achieved all-out superiority over the French fleet, for most of the time after 1702 it provided a formidable deterrent to invasion. Ships could, and did, slip through the British cordons, but a fleet escorting a large number of transports could never have evaded full-scale naval battle.

In 1744 Prince Charles Edward had hoped to secure the help of a French army, embarking for England from Dunkirk, but the arrival of a strong British fleet, plus a tempest, effectually prevented the French transports from sailing. The Prince decided to take his chances and in July 1745, in one of the French ships which got through the British blockade, he reached Scotland. He had with him a few men, scant military supplies and little money.

Competent contemporary observers estimated the Highland potential of armed men as 32,000.[1] The Prince's army never exceeded 8,000. Of the remaining three-quarters of the clansmen, some clearly waited to see the outcome, some were indifferent, and others—such as the northern clans, Mackays, Sutherlands and Munroes—were on the Government side. However, Charles's small army defeated a poorly composed British army at Prestonpans, near Edinburgh, on 21 September 1745. In November he evaded a British army under General Wade, advancing from Newcastle; then, taking his march through Cumberland, the Prince captured Carlisle and marched down to Derby.

No support had come from the French, and the other source from which the Prince had expected recruits—the body of English Jacobites—produced no more than 300 men who were formed into an English regiment. The old Catholic Jacobite families of North Wales, Lancashire and Cheshire did nothing. The Government in London had taken strong measures. It had rapidly recalled troops from Flanders, where the British were fighting the French, and had also summoned to its aid some Dutch troops under a treaty with Holland which allowed for such supply. In all, by the beginning of December 1745, there were 30,000 regular troops in three armies in England: General Wade's army in the north, an army near London, and, most formidable, a third under the Duke of Cumberland, George II's soldier son, which was not more than two days' march from Derby. In addition, the Government had called out the militia in each county, though it had proved completely ineffective during the Highlanders' march on Derby.

At Manchester, Prince Charles in high spirits had discussed the manner of his entry into London, what clothes he should wear, and whether he should ride or walk. His chiefs were not so optimistic, and particularly his general, Lord George Murray. In a council of war held on 5 December it was decided, after long and bitter opposition on the part of the Prince, to retreat to Scotland on the 6 December and this was completed on 20 December 1745, the Prince's twenty-fifth birthday. The Highland army travelled light, and was thus able to evade the much slower-moving British forces. It appears, too, that most of the Highlanders rode back, commandeering horses as they went. In the retreat they were sometimes stoned by mobs, and stragglers were murdered or imprisoned. Once or twice bodies of the militia appeared and fired pistols.[2]

Several places in Scotland had held out for George II, notably Edinburgh Castle and the forts in the Great Glen. An army under General Hawley gathered to recover Scotland and there was a battle at Falkirk between this force and the Highlanders which gave the Prince a victory, though it did not, as at Prestonpans, destroy the regular force. Meanwhile, small bodies of French troops had landed at Stonehaven, Montrose and Peterhead, and fresh Highlanders were mustering under Lord Strathallan at Perth.

It was decided to retreat to the north-western Highlands, to conduct guerilla warfare during the winter and to come out for open battle in the spring of 1746. What, in fact, happened was that on 16 April 1746, the Highland army, in the worst position for a clan onslaught, was defeated at Culloden by the Duke of Cumberland's troops with very heavy losses.

The Rising was over but the consequences were to be felt for 200 years. Clearly the strength of the '45 had been the Highland clans. There had been nothing resembling a massive French landing in the Prince's support; 500–600 men at the most. The English Jacobites had done nothing beyond the recruitment of not more than 300 men, while three gentlemen from Wales brought their own persons and possibly some good wishes for the Prince from the old landed families.

In fact, the Rising proved that a contemporary observer,

Dr Samuel Johnson, was perfectly right when he said that if it came to a vote the Stuarts would be restored and the Hanoverians sent away, but that if anyone in England had to do more for the Stuarts than vote for them, nothing would happen. 'Poor young fellow', Johnson remarked of the Prince, but remained completely loyal to the reigning king and accepted a pension from George III.

None the less the successes of the Prince's army had caused great alarm in England. There had been a run on the Bank of England and a yacht had been prepared for removal of Hanoverian family valuables to the Continent. George II, who was an experienced soldier, did not share in what must have been a panic in London. It is idle to speculate on what would have happened if the Prince had continued his march towards London. Isolated in a country where no man cried 'Godspeed' to his proclamations of James VIII, he was very unlikely to have defeated two regular armies. His chiefs, completely disillusioned by the failure of the English Jacobites to come to their aid, saw the imminent dangers of a forward march, and their thoughts may well have been those expressed in the words of Fergus MacIvor, wise with the hind sight which history gives,

. . . that, as on former occasions, the heading, hanging and forfeiting will chiefly fall to the lot of the Lowland gentry; that they will be left secure in their poverty and their fastnesses there, according to their proverb, 'to listen to the wind upon the hill till the waters abate'. But they will be disappointed; they have been too often troublesome to be so repeatedly passed over, and this time John Bull has been too heartily frightened to recover his good humour for some time. The Hanoverian ministers . . . since there is neither rising in England nor assistance from France, will deserve the gallows as fools if they leave a single clan in the Highlands in a situation to be again troublesome to Government. Ay, they will make root and branch work, I warrant them. *Waverley*, ch 59.

The above is Sir Walter Scott's view given in 1805, sixty years after the '45, but it is a fair summing-up. For many centuries the condition of the Highlands had been that of an area where the law of Scotland had been very imperfectly obeyed. Several expedients were employed to bring the Highlands to order, but none was effective. The Union of the Crowns of England and Scotland in 1603 led to the pacification of the Borders, the other disturbed area of Scotland, but the Highlands were not reduced to order. The Union of England and Scotland into Great Britain in 1707 made the position of tribal districts incongruous within a modern state, yet twice after that date the Highlanders were in rebellion against the Government, in the 1715 Rising and the '45. After the earlier of these the Government attempted several precautionary measures, such as the building of roads into the Highlands, and Acts for disarming the clansmen. The roads actually helped the march of Prince Charlie's men, and the weapons surrendered were either worn-out old arms, or were sent in by clans loyal to the Government. For thirty years there was an uneasy peace in the Highlands. Clan wars ceased in the late seventeenth century, but depredations against Lowland landowners continued right up to and through the '45. It was to prevent this 'blackmail' that the Independent Companies of Highlanders were recruited, the nucleus of the famous Black Watch Regiment.

The fright which came to England (and to Lowland Scotland) produced the result mentioned above by Fergus. The feudal heritable jurisdictions of the Highland chiefs and landlords were abolished, which was logical enough, but another consequence of the Government's fear, understandable but by no means excusable, was the pacification of the Highlands after Culloden. Tacitus, the Roman historian who wrote the description of the first battle recorded between Highlanders and Lowlanders, put into the mouth of the Highland chief, Galgacus, the sentence 'Solitudinem faciunt, pacem appellant',[3] referring to the Romans. It would not have been a bad description of the pacification of the Highlands after 1746. The atrocities committed by Cumberland's army make horrible reading, but they could be said to have achieved their purpose, for never again was there a Highland rising or any warlike action in the Highlands. A particularly vindictive Government measure introduced at this time was the prohibition by statute, under the pain of very severe penalties, of the wearing of Highland dress. This ban existed for thirty-five years until 1782.

After the brutal treatment of the clansmen by the British Army a fate in some ways even worse befell them. Often the punishment of the Highlanders came from other Scotsmen, and there were several Scottish regiments on the Government side at Culloden. The Highland Clearances which occurred in 1782–1820 and 1840–54 were almost entirely the work of Highland chiefs and ducal landlords. They preferred sheep to men, and the present partially depopulated condition of the Highlands stems from these clearances.

Many of the Highlanders were forcibly removed from their homelands, and large settlements of clansmen were made in Canada and in the United States. It says a great deal for the inherent loyalty of the clansman to his chief that the clan system should have survived this rough uprooting of men from the glens where they were born and where their ancestors had lived from time untold. It also says much for the essential gentleness of the Highland Gael that the men in the Highlands did not resist the evictions. Brave in their chiefs' quarrels, they were passive in their own. They left it to their womenfolk to offer resistance to the police, and later to the soldiers who were used to remove the clansfolk from their lands.

The Clearances completed the work begun by Cumberland's soldiers. Clans which had taken no part in the '45 might escape, though not always; clans loyal to the Government were relatively safe. Once the clearance policy had been adopted, no distinction was made between loyalty to Stuart or Hanoverian.

So by the first half of the nineteenth century the end had come for what had really been a tribal and patriarchal society in which, in theory, the chief of a clan was united to his clansmen by blood ties. The land had belonged to the whole clan and was merely administered by the chief. In the course of 700 years, from the eleventh to the eighteenth centuries, many changes had occurred in this ancient system. Forms of feudalism, under which the land belonged to the lord who subinfeudated it to his vassals, began to intrude into the patriarchal way of life. Later, the more modern legal concept of land ownership, witnessed by deeds—'sheepskin grants'—with regular leases, made its way among the Highlanders. Still, in 1745, enough of the old patriarchal system remained to bear witness to the original meaning of the word clan, ie, children.

The ancient way of life which had been known in the Highlands from time long anterior to the consolidation of the Scottish kingdom thus disappeared after the suppression of the '45. The Clearances ensured the dispersion of the clansmen all over the world. Then occurred a strange metamorphosis.

The Scots had been originally a tribe from Ireland who had settled in Argyllshire and the neighbouring islands. By a series of accidents, their name became applicable to the whole realm and people of Scotland. For many centuries, however, a distinction was made, by Scots themselves, between people in the Highlands and in the Lowlands. The former were styled 'Redshanks', 'wild Scots', and 'savages', and they spoke a language quite different from English. Originally the Highlanders' tongue, Gaelic, had been spoken far down into the Lowlands and even in what is now the Border country. Gradually over the centuries from the time of Malcolm Canmore (his nickname is Gaelic for 'Big Head') and his English queen, Princess, later St Margaret, English displaced Gaelic and feudalism made inroads on the clan system. In 1286 the Celtic dynasty ended with Alexander III. The claimants to the throne, the houses of Balliol and Bruce who in turn became rulers of Scotland, were of Norman origin in the male line, though they descended on the female side from the old dynasty. They were typical of the great baronial families, having properties in England and Scotland and owing allegiance to the kings of both countries. In the sequel, the Bruces won and within two generations the Stuarts, their heirs through the female line, succeeded. By this time, the fourteenth century, the Anglicisation of Scotland was complete as far as the Lowlands were concerned. This may seem strange in view of the tremendous struggle for Scottish freedom which culminated at Bannockburn in 1314, but although the greater clans fought on Bruce's side in that battle, the make-up of Scotland thereafter became less and less Celtic and the trend always nearer to England.

With each century the rift between Highland and Lowland inhabitants became more pronounced—in speech, in clothing, in way of life and, with the Reformation, also in religion. Many of the clans, especially in the Isles, adhered to Catholicism, while the rest of Scotland devoted itself to Protestantism, making yet another link with England and one which finally broke up the 'Auld Alliance' between Scotland and France. Then, too, from the late seventeenth century onward Lowland Scotland, like England, was a relatively law-abiding country in which men settled disputes in lawcourts and not by resort to arms. In the Highlands, the clansmen kept their weapons and as late as 1690 fought out a private war with a clan battle.

Thus, by the time of the '45 the way of life in the Highlands was an anomaly. Instead of being allowed to die out peacefully, or be phased out by economic pressure, the system met with a violent end. It is probable that the support given to the Stuarts by some of the Highland chiefs—under Montrose in the '15 and under Graham of Claverhouse, in the '45—sprang partly from respect for the King as Chief of Chiefs, and also from an instinct that the old ways of clan life could be protected and preserved only by a Stuart restoration.

With the complete downfall of the Stuart cause and the pacification of the Highlands the whole clan past might well have beome simply a chapter in history, albeit a romantic one. Their fate could have been comparable with that of the American Indians who, after more than 350 years of struggle with the Whites, were defeated and their survivors shut up in reserves. The Indians had had their own culture and tried to keep it. They had won many battles against the Americans but they lacked unity, and though many American writers now condemn their treatment by the Whites, it is evident that the only future for the Indian is by assimilation to White culture.[4]

Something similar to the position of the Indians on their reserves might have been the lot of the clans had they been allowed to remain in their glens. The proscription of the Highland garb made it popular, once the ban on its use was removed in 1782. Tartan, plaids, belted plaids and the kilt came into vogue, and after the visit of George IV to Scotland in 1822, the first sovereign to go there since Charles II, Highland clothes became the rage and everybody who was anybody had to wear tartan and the kilt. The King's visit was ably stage-managed by Sir Walter Scott, then at the height of his fame, and will be recounted in its proper place.

There was also a vast increase in interest in everything else connected with the Highlands. Queen Victoria and the Prince Consort built Balmoral, it became customary to refer to 'Royal Deeside', and the Queen later had a Highland ghillie, John Brown, as a favourite attendant. The Highlands, forcibly cleared of the majority of the inhabitants, now became fashionable and its mountains, hitherto ignored, became 'beautiful', 'magnificent' and 'awe inspiring'. English visitors poured into Scotland and more especially into the Highlands, many of them influenced by Sir Walter Scott's writings since most readers like to see the scenes in which their favourite novels are set.

So it came about that at the very time when the clan system had been broken up and most of the clansmen deported to North America, Highlander became synonymous with Scot. Today, everyone is familiar with plays, films, novels, advertisements and television in which the Scot is portrayed in a kilt, speaking English, of course, and in many cases having no blood or cultural connection with the Highlands. The term 'Sassenach', heard as applied by Lowlanders to Englishmen, is a Gaelic word and was for a long time used by the Gael of persons who lived in the Lowlands. That one man lived in Midlothian and another in Middlesex seemed to the Highlander of 1745 of little importance. Both were Lowlanders to him—foreigners, as he to them.

Gaeldom died but yet it triumphed. To outward appearance the Scottish nation became Highland. Lord Macaulay, who died in 1860, wrote with his usual eloquence about the transformation that had taken place in the Saxon's views of the Highlander, and that vast change has, if anything, grown even greater in the twentieth century. Books written in the early 1900s about the clans show clan maps covering only the mountainous areas of Scotland, whereas similar books today show all Scotland divided into clan areas.[5] On the London stage, the knightly and noble Douglas of Shakespeare's *Henry IV* (Part 1) has been seen garbed as a Highlander among the mail-clad warriors at Shrewsbury! Leaving all fancies apart and all modern delusions, let us now examine the true story of the Gael.

2   The Origin of the Gael

THE EARLY HISTORY of most nations is obscure since, if their origin is at all distant in time, it began before there were written documents. Even when the latter exist they may well be sparse in number, vague in wording and often the writers were concerned with subjects of little interest to the modern researcher, while being tantalisingly brief on matters important to him. The United States of America can document its history from the settlement of Virginia under James I; similarly with all the countries in the Americas and Australasia, but in Europe this is quite impossible and Scotland is no exception.

Archaeology, along with linguistic study, can give many indications as to the movements of peoples and their settlements in the British Isles, and these sources of information considerably augment what we are able to learn from the classical writers. The Greeks and the Romans were the first students of anthropology in Europe. They liked to know as much as possible about the races of barbarians, as they called all European peoples apart from themselves, and modern historical writing would be seriously handicapped without the works of writers such as Herodotus, Julius Caesar, Strabo and Tacitus. With their aid, and our much more recent archaeological knowledge, we can dimly discern the extensive movements of races in the early centuries BC. When the history of Britain in the documented sense is opened by the *Commentaries* of Julius Caesar, we find what we should now call England inhabited by tribes whom, for want of a better term, are called Celts. They were akin to the people of Gaul and some of the tribes whom Caesar knew there, like the Belgae, had only recently sent colonists into southern Britain. Indeed, the kinship between the tribes of Britain and of Gaul (and the aid the British might render to their kinsfolk) was the ostensible reason for Caesar's invasions in 55 and 54 BC.

Caesar's account opened up southern Britain to the knowledge of the Romans, but it could only raise the curtain on a small part of the country. It was not then known whether Britain was an island, or if it joined up with the northern lands beyond the German Ocean. Nearly a century passed before the Romans again invaded Britain, in AD 43, but when they did their progress was comparatively rapid. The Roman Governor of Britain between AD 78–85, Gnaeus Julius Agricola, the father-in-law of the historian Tacitus,[1] pushed the Roman boundaries much further northward than his predecessors had contemplated. During the year 81 Agricola advanced as far as the Firths of Clyde and Forth, which were then known as Clota and Bodotra. The narrow 'waist' of Scotland at this point was then occupied, fortified and garrisoned by the Romans. There does not seem to have been much opposition and the next year Agricola, whose army was accompanied by his fleet, sailed among the western islands, probably Arran and near Kintyre. From western Scotland he contemplated Ireland, and held the same view of its relationship to Britain which Julius Caesar had had of Britain's connection with Gaul. The contemplation of freedom in a nearby island—discernible on clear days from Galloway—might keep the Britons restive under Roman rule, and Agricola could have counted upon the aid of one of the native kings of Ireland who had been driven out and was prepared to play a Quisling-like role in Ireland if reinstated. But Agricola, unlike Caesar, had a master in Rome, the Emperor Domitian who adhered to the rule laid down by Augustus not to extend the boundaries of the Empire, and so the Irish were left to their freedom for another 1,100 years. When Henry II obtained permission from the Pope to invade Ireland, he had the services of an exiled Irish king. The Roman failure to invade Ireland has been lamented by some writers, particularly Hilaire Belloc and, as will be seen, the close connection between the Irish and the Scottish Gael does derive a considerable influence from this fact.

In northern Britain, however, Agricola was allowed to proceed, and in AD 83 he invaded the land north of Clyde and Forth with both army and fleet. He passed the estuary of the

Tay (Taum, or Tanaum, is the name given by Tacitus and it is interesting to note how old is this name and that of Clyde). He had a large army of some 30,000 men with him, but one of his legions, the IXth, was fiercely attacked by the Caledonians. The Romans were victorious, and both sides prepared during the winter for a decisive struggle. In 84 the Romans marched to a place which they called *Mons Graupius* and which is not to be confused with the Grampian Mountains.[3] Its site is unknown, but it was probably in eastern Scotland and certainly in hilly country. The northern tribes had acted like the southern Britons in Caesar's time and elected a leader, Calgacus, to direct their operations. They mustered in great strength but were completely defeated by Agricola. The losses are described as being 10,000 of the Caledonians, and only 360 of the Romans. The northern parts of Scotland were then densely forested and the Caledonian defeat merely meant that they withdrew into almost inaccessible country. Agricola's fleet circumnavigated Britain, thus proving it to be an island, but whatever plans he may have had for further conquest were frustrated by his recall to Rome in 85.

The Romans never conquered Scotland beyond Clyde and Forth. Remains of Roman camps are found in the Lowlands, and the Antonine Wall stretched across the 'waist' but was not so formidable an obstacle as the Hadrian Wall between Solway and Tyne (built in 121) which, as long as it was adequately garrisoned, could not be overpassed by the northern tribes. The next attempt to conquer the north came in the year 208, when the Emperor Severus, an African who had made himself ruler of the Roman Empire by force, campaigned against the Caledonians and reached the Moray Firth.[4] According to some accounts he lost 40,000 men in the process. Crippled by gout, he retired to York whence he issued orders to his generals to exterminate the Caledonians. On his death, however, his sons called off the campaign and the tribes of the Highlands were once again left alone.

Later, in the fourth century, when the Roman Empire was verging on its decline, Hadrian's Wall was inadequately garrisoned and the tribes broke through, ravaging Britain as far south as Kent. Order was restored by the father of the future Emperor Theodosius and the northern tribes driven back to their own country. The Roman legions were recalled to the Continent in 410–11, and the Romano-British provincials were left to their own devices.

Who were the Caledonians? Celts is an easy and almost inevitable answer, and passages from Caesar and Tacitus have been pressed into service and worn threadbare by successive authors. Almost all the classical writers from Aristotle to Procopius[5] have been searched for scraps of information. Our certain knowledge is that several layers of races penetrated to Britain but that the Celts, in various groupings, occupied the country, ruling over or ignoring pockets of the population left from earlier migrations. According to Tacitus's account of Agricola's campaign in the north, the Caledonians far outnumbered his men, so that if this is correct the population must have been very large then, whereas, in the historic period, the Highland clans seem not to have exceeded some 130,000 persons. The dense forestation of Scotland no doubt afforded habitat for very large quantities of game, including wild cattle and red deer, and these, with copious supplies of fish, may have supported a larger population than in the seventeenth and eighteenth centuries.

Speculation is anyway of little value. By the time of Rome's decline in Britain, the northern invaders of the province are familiar to most people from schoolbook memories as the Picts and the Scots. Of the latter mention will come presently. The Picts, the *picti* or painted men, had an extensive domain from Caithness to the Forth. They were the fierce Caledonians whom the Romans did not subdue, and had a culture of their own, shown in many sculptures depicting men and animals. They had their own language, probably a form of Gaelic, which has disappeared along with their genealogies and any possible records. They traced succession through the mother's line and matrilineal accession to the throne of Pictland was a phenomenon not peculiar to them. They have disappeared into the Scottish people, not annihilated but absorbed.

Anyone who has studied the surviving Celtic tongues—Irish, Gaelic, Welsh, Manx, Breton—knows that these languages differ very greatly from English and the other branches of the Germanic family. Philologists can, of course, bring them within the Indo-Germanic scheme of tongues, but to the general observer the differences between Celtic and Germanic argue a long separation of their speakers from the original stock. In turn, differences arose in the speech between the various Celtic races, though these were not of great importance. The Venerable Bede (673–735) in his *Ecclesiastical History of the English People* (ch 1) stated that Britain had formerly been called Albion, and that in his time it was inhabited by five nations, the English, Britons, Scots, Picts and Latins. The last can be ignored since the name refers only to the cultivated speech used by scholars. As far as Scotland is concerned, the four nations mentioned by Bede constituted four parts of the Scottish people, to which can be added the Norsemen who lived in the Hebrides, Orkneys and Shetlands, and who arrived after Bede's time.

The Picts had a tradition, according to Bede, that they had come from Scythia, in Asia. Other traditions of this type appear much later in Scottish history, including claims that the Scots had originated far to the east, in Asia. Curiously enough, reliefs of Pictish warriors on Orkney gravestones have a decidedly Assyrian appearance, so there may be substance in the tradition after all.[6]

Of the five ingredients in the making of Scotland, the distribution was as follows. Strathclyde, that is Galloway in south-western Scotland, was inhabited by the Britons, ie, Celtic folk of the same type as Caesar's opponents in the south. In common with the rest of the Romano-Britons, they had been pushed or penned into a corner of Britain by the fifth-century invasion of Angles, Saxons and Jutes, tribes from Germany and Denmark. The latter had become known by Bede's time as the English people and their language as English, the first literary monuments to which date from about 700. They conquered the old Roman province of Britain and converted it into England. In the process they obliterated the older inhabitants, killing many, assimilating some and driving the rest into the physically more difficult parts of the country—Wales, Cornwall and Strathclyde. The story of the Highland clans could thus be written as that of the gradual encroachment of the English and their language upon Celtic areas. In the course of this struggle, Cornwall has been absorbed into England and its language has died; Strathclyde has been divided between England and Scotland, and Gaelic died out there many centuries ago. Manx is nearly extinct as a spoken language in Man, Gaelic is gradually dying in the Scottish Highlands, and in Wales Welsh is spoken by not more than 25 per cent of the inhabitants. In Ireland, the Irish language has the official backing of the Republican Government and is obligatory in certain employments. The story of Scotland is largely that of the steady advance of everything English.

When Bede wrote, the Picts were still a powerful force with their own monarchy. Who, then, were the Scots who have given their name to the whole country? They came about the third century of the Christian era from northern Ireland and settled in Argyll, Kintyre and the western islands. Their kingdom was known as Dalriada, which they named after a district in Antrim where their royal family had originated. At first they were outnumbered by the more powerful Picts, but in the course of 300 years they spread up the Great Glen (where the Caledonian Canal now is) and reached from Argyll to Strathclyde. They had the normal succession in the royal house from father to son, and they intermarried with the Pictish royal house, though this did not prevent frequent wars between the Picts and Scots. The latter remained quite closely connected with their kinsfolk in northern Ireland, and the Scottish leader in Dalriada even acknowledged the suzerainty of the older Irish line. About AD 500, Fergus MacErc and his brothers Angus and Lorne brought over fresh bodies of settlers but about the middle of the sixth century the Scots were very much depressed by contrast with the Picts, to whom they had lost several battles. The decisive turning point for the Scots was the arrival of St Columba from Ireland.

The Irish were converted to Christianity by St Patrick (incidentally, not an Irishman but a western Briton) in the fifth century. They embraced the faith with ardour and sent forth missionaries to other parts of the British Isles and all over western Europe. Indeed, between the sixth and eighth centuries, Ireland merited the title of the island of saints and scholars. Learning and the arts flourished and to the labours of the Irish missionaries many lands owed their Christian faith. Prominent among these was the great St Columba, who came from Ireland in 563 and established his church centre on the island of Iona. He converted the Scots to Christianity and also succeeded in putting fresh vigour into their monarchy. Other Irish and Scottish teachers brought the faith to northern England. The Northumbrian kingdom stretched up into the Lowlands of Scotland, taking in the Lothians and giving an English name, Edwin's burgh, to Dunedin. The northern English kingdom might have taken firm hold of the Scottish Lowlands but for the fact that the southern Picts had defeated the Northumbrians at the battle of Nectansmere (possibly in Angus) in 685.

St Columba's influence extended to the Picts, who became Christians in and after his time. Long before this, the Strathclyde Britons had been converted by St Ninian and his disciples. In what became the English kingdoms of the Heptarchy, Christianity had been ousted by the pagan Angles and Saxons, who were subsequently converted partly by the labours of St Augustine, sent from Rome to Kent in 597 by Pope Gregory the Great, and partly by Irish and Scottish missionaries working in the north.

Thus, the four nations named by Bede—English, Britons, Picts and Scots—who were to make up Scotland, had by AD 600–700 one important thing in common, their religion. But the fifth racial component of Scotland, that of the Vikings or Norsemen, was for long completely hostile to religion and culture. In the latter part of the eighth century the Scandinavians stirred in their homelands and moved out to make a lasting impact on the world. The Swedish Vikings went into Finland and Russia, establishing the royal line of Rurik in the latter country. The Danish and Norwegian Vikings spread out northward and westward. Of their attacks on England and France, the Danelaw in the one and the province of Normandy in the other were the result. Ireland was badly affected by them. They established footholds in the ports, and although they failed to dominate the whole country they destroyed most of its splendid culture.

On Scotland, the Norsemen had an equally important effect. Their voyages and actions extended from the eighth to the eleventh centuries and for a long time were purely destructive. In 793 they sacked Lindisfarne, Holy Island; Iona knew their longships, and in 839 they defeated a combination of Picts and

Scots. The earlier phase of destruction was followed, as else-where, by settlement and colonisation. The Hebrides, the Orkneys and the Shetlands were taken over by the Norse. They claimed all the islands from Iceland to Man (hence the Norse name 'Sodor', or 'South', in the full style of the Anglican bishop of Man—Sodor and Man). Nor was their claim un-justified, and not until 1263, at the battle of Largs, did the Scots eliminate the Viking menace to their western islands and mainland. By the treaty of Perth in 1266 the Norwegian king gave over Man and the western isles to Scotland in return for a cash settlement, but two hundred years were to pass before the Orkneys and Shetlands became Scottish. James III of Scotland in 1468 arranged to marry Margaret, daughter of the King of Denmark and Norway, and when her dowry, for which the Orkneys and Shetlands had been pledged, was not paid the Scots king annexed the two groups of islands. Only towards the end of the fifteenth century was Scotland geographically complete as we know it now.

Back in the ninth century, the Norse invasion of Scotland produced, as it did in England, a consolidation of the kingdom. In 843, only four years after the Scots and Picts had been beaten by the Vikings, Kenneth MacAlpine, the Scottish king, became also King of the Picts. The kings of Scotland are reckoned from him.

The Irish tribe of the Scots had succeeded in taking over the country. Known previously as Alba or Alban (possibly con-nected with Albion), it was now known as Scotland, and the people as Scots. The Scottish kings were for a long time buried in Iona, but when Kenneth MacAlpine became King of the Scots and Picts, he was crowned as such at Scone, in Perthshire, on the ancient Stone of Destiny. Scone was the sacred place of the Pictish kingdom and became the capital of the now united realm in place of Dunstaffnage, in Argyll, which had been the centre of the Scottish line of kings. It has often been said that the stone was that on which the High Kings of Ireland were crowned at Tara and, even more remarkable, that the Irish Coronation Stone was that on which Jacob rested his head at Bethel. Geological examination, however, has proved that the stone is of the Lower Old Red Sandstone, ie, Scottish stone from the vicinity of Scone. For nearly 700 years now it has lain beneath the coronation chair of the English kings in Westminster Abbey, to which it was brought by Edward I in 1296.[7]

During the time of union of Picts and Scots many acts of cruelty, treachery and bloodshed took place. It is said for instance, that the Seven Earls of Alba were murdered by King Kenneth MacAlpine after he had got them into his power. Many similar actions mark the course of Scottish history, and also of clan history.[8] So free indeed was the Highlanders' use of sword and dirk on such occasions, and so unusual their style of dress, that their southern neighbours were wont to refer to them as savages or wild Scots, though, in fact, the Lowlanders themselves were often guilty of acts of extreme barbarity towards the Highlanders. Among the latter, several of the older and simpler virtues were commonly observed. Like the Arabs of the deserts, the Highlander had a high regard for the duties of hospitality, and those who became his guests and ate of his salt were assured of safety and protection. Loyalty was ever a great Highland virtue, even when it may have seemed misplaced; loyalty to the death to the chief, and loyalty to the same degree to the Chief of Chiefs, the Stuart King, as was shown in the clan ruin of the '45. Observance of an oath, if sufficiently solemn, as when taken on the dirk, was sacred, and the marriage bond was respected among clansmen. Their extreme ferocity in warfare was not paralleled in private, where the best qualities of a soldier—gentleness in peace and extreme bravery in war— were exemplified. They were not irreligious, though their opportunities of church attendance were limited, and they did not, as a rule, adhere to the Presbyterianism of their Lowland neighbours. Superstition, in the form of a belief in fairies and other supernatural beings, and in monsters like water kelpies, was certainly rife among the clansmen but, as Charles Kingsley says, they were mainly healthy beliefs which did little harm and were dictated largely by the grandeur of the scenery.

This is somewhat to anticipate, and for the scope of the present chapter it is enough to note that, from 843, the Highlands and the land down to the Forth formed one kingdom of Scotland. Strathclyde was incorporated in the growing realm between 1018 and 1034. Duncan, the grandson and heir of Malcolm II (1005–34), succeeded to the throne of Strathclyde in 1018, when its last native ruler died childless. Thus, when Duncan succeeded his grandfather in 1034, the limits of the Scottish mainland territory were very much what they are today, because the English Lothians had also in 1018 been taken over by the King of Scots.

The monarchy of this Celtic line lasted from 843 to 1286. It was a realm of clans and largely Gaelic-speaking, except in the Lothians in the south-east. Under the clan system the land belonged to the whole clan, unlike the feudal system in which the lord owned the land and let it out to vassals. The chief was the father of his clan and many of the clansmen were indeed related to the chief by blood. Most of the great clans had septs, that is branches or sub-divisions, coming very often from sons and bearing different surnames. While the theory of blood relationship was held, and was true of the different branches of a chief's family, it did not apply to all of what may be called the rank and file of clansmen. There were always in the Highlands men without a clan, the most important of several reasons for this being the break-up of a clan following defeat in battle. Men from such broken clans were glad to come under the protection of a chief and to be allowed to use his surname. Even quite late in the seventeenth century a whole clan, the MacGregors, was outlawed and its surname proscribed, so that the famous Rob Roy MacGregor took the name of Campbell in order to be under the protection of the Duke of Argyll. Blood connection with the main chief's family cannot and could not be proved for all clansmen merely because they bore the chief's surname.

It may be remarked in passing that the Duncan mentioned above as succeeding to the throne of Strachclyde in 1018, is the original of Shakespeare's Duncan in his *Macbeth*, though the Macbeth of history is a rather different character from the dramatist's creation. Having slain Duncan in battle, Macbeth reigned wisely for seventeen years, even going on a pilgrimage to Rome. He was eventually defeated and killed by Duncan's son, Malcolm III.

3 The History of the Celtic Monarchy

THE OFT-QUOTED saying about the happiness of a country which has no history may be applied to the Highland clans. Not until the twelfth century does the history of what was for ages the greatest of the clans—the Macdonalds, whose chiefs were Lords of the Isles—come into the narrative of Scottish affairs. Then we find Somerled, described by one of the most careful clan historians as 'the progenitor of the Macdonalds', who, 'by his marriage and by a series of successful wars attained a position of independence and power, which was little restricted by the nominal suzerainty of Norway.'[1] Somerled, who died in battle against the Scottish king Malcolm IV in 1164, was the son of Gillebride, of whom a great authority (Sir Thomas Innes of Learney, Lord Lyon, 1945–69) remarked 'The history of Gillebride, who lived about the end of the 10th and the beginning of the 11th century, is involved in obscurity.'[2]

The history of the Lords of the Isles will come later and the above is quoted only to show that even the greatest of clans could not trace the origins of its progenitor to anything like the lengths to which Welsh princes and, even more, Irish kings could validly go. In Wales there are about a dozen of the old princely families with proven genealogies each of a millennium. Wales has no genealogical connection with the Scottish Highlands, but as both Welsh and Gaels are of the same Celtic stock, and as Celtic races have usually been interested in pedigree, it is a little surprising that Welsh genealogical trees should be so much longer than those of the Highlands. The Irish royal pedigrees are renowned for their length and when all due allowance has been made for scepticism about Hibernian tales, most of the royal lines can be accepted for some two or three generations before St Patrick.[3] This gives a start for Irish royal pedigrees about AD 400, the period in which the celebrated Niall of the Nine Hostages was killed. That the Highland chiefs did not rival the genealogies of their Irish kinsfolk seems strange, especially as Irish connections and influence on the Highlanders lasted so long. As late as the seventeenth century the Highland language is commonly referred to as Irish. In the matter of clothing, too, as will be seen in due course, Irish influence did not end until, at the close of Elizabeth's reign, the conquest of Ireland and the suppression of rebellions dealt a very severe blow to Irish culture.

That the Highland clans cannot demonstrate a long history—and in the majority of families do not even claim it—can be seen from the pedigrees printed in *Burke's Landed Gentry* and *Burke's Peerage*, where the pedigree has the family's approval. Even so illustrious a name as that of the MacGregors cannot be documented before 1390, though they claim, probably correctly, descent to the middle of the twelfth century, and even from Kenneth MacAlpine, whence they are often known as the Clan Alpine. No clan has been as persecuted as much as the MacGregors and their records may well have been destroyed, but other powerful and important clans do not begin their chiefs' lineage much before the thirteenth century, which, set against the long pedigrees of the Welsh and Irish, is not great antiquity. This is borne out by entries in Sir Thomas Innes's edition of Adam's work, *The Clans, Septs and Regiments of the Scottish Highlands*, for MacDougall (derived in the twelfth century from Clan Donald); Macfie, 'of their early history nothing is known'; Macinnes, 'remarkably little of this clan's history is recorded'; Mackintosh, a very renowned clan, later twelfth century; Macintyre, 1300–1400; Mackenzie, 'first ancestor... of whom there is authentic charter evidence' lived in 1362; Maclean, twelfth to thirteenth century, and Macpherson, 1173.

The interest of the above is that, in writing clan history, most historians begin with the contests with the Scottish Crown waged by the clan Donald, the chiefs of which were Lords of the Isles. These began in the twelfth century and did not end until nearly the sixteenth. For the present chapter, concern is with the earlier period.

The 'Young Malcolm', before whose feet Macbeth refused to fall (in Shakespeare's play), became Malcolm III. He was known as Ceann Mor (Anglicised to Canmore) the 'Big Headed', and reigned from 1058 to 1093. His reign marked a great change in Scotland's constitution for it saw the beginning of the feudalisation and Anglicisation of Scotland. Malcolm had lived as a child and young man at the court of the English king, Edward the Confessor. Neither the language nor the habits of the English were strange to him but it was not his early upbringing which had the greatest influence upon him. This came from his second marriage with the Princess Margaret, sister of Edgar the Atheling, the true heir to the English throne.

Edgar was in some ways one of the most unfortunate princes in history, although he does not appear to have grieved overmuch about his lost throne, and after a varied series of adventures succeeded in dying in peace at the age of about seventy. He was the grandson of King Edmund II, Edmund Ironside, the last hero of the royal house of Wessex, who fought Canute to a standstill and made terms with him, only to die in mysterious circumstances in 1017, a few weeks after the division of England between himself and Canute. Edmund's young children were sent abroad, with instructions to their hosts from Canute that they should be murdered. These directions were mercifully not carried out and the children were reared in Hungary where one died, but the other, known as Edward the Exile, received the King of Hungary's daughter in marriage. Many years later, Edward the Confessor, who was deliberately childless, bethought him of his half-brother and sent for the Exile. When the latter reached England some strange and unexplained circumstances kept him from seeing his uncle, and he died soon after his arrival. His son Edgar was too young in those rough times to be made King on the death of Edward the Confessor, and the latter's chief minister, Harold Godwinson, succeeded to the throne as Harold II in 1066. The Norman invasion followed and Duke William became King William the Conqueror, having defeated and slain Harold at Hastings. There was no rule of succession to the throne by next-of-kin which would have brought in young Edgar, and William, though he always relied on force of arms, was careful to use every pretext of law. He claimed the English throne on the ground that his cousin the Confessor had promised it to him. In addition, a few years before the Conquest, William had got Harold into his power and forced him to swear an oath of allegiance to him. Consequently when Harold became King, William at once declared him a perjured usurper, and was very skilful in securing the support of the Papacy.

After Harold's death, the English Council, or Witan, proclaimed young Edgar the Atheling (the title borne by English princes) as King. Not more than a month later the official resistance to William collapsed and among those who came to William's camp to offer him the Crown was Edgar.

William treated Edgar kindly and gave him estates as compensation for his loss of the kingdom. He seems never to have anticipated any trouble from the Atheling and, being a good judge of men, he probably recognised that the neutral quality of the Atheling's character would prevent him from ever leading a national revolt. It is certain that neither William I nor William II ever harmed the Atheling, although the latter was in and out of rebellion against Norman rule more than once.[4]

How, then, could so colourless a man have influenced the course of Scottish history? He could not and did not, but he had two sisters, Margaret and Christina. The latter became a nun, but Margaret was a woman of outstanding character who left a decisive mark on Scotland. It might well have been her persuasion as an elder sister that led Edgar to flee from William the Conqueror's court and take refuge with Malcolm. This was in 1067 and in 1068 Margaret became Malcolm's second wife. She was beautiful, she was educated (Malcolm was illiterate), and she was profoundly attached to the Catholic Church. Although she had been brought up in Hungary, she was English in outlook and deeply sympathetic to the English who were suffering under the Norman yoke. Already after Hastings, English people were beginning to seek shelter in Scotland, and after Margaret became Malcolm's queen, the Scottish court was wide open to receive English refugees.

With the Atheling we have no more to do, but his sister Margaret began the transformation of the rough Scottish kingdom. In the first place the influx of Englishmen profoundly affected the character of Scotland. Not only did many great men seek asylum with the Scots, but large numbers of lesser folk fled into the Lothians. There they found people speaking the same language and, combining with the latter, greatly increased the English character of the district. The surname of Inglis means 'the Englishman', and it is often found in the southernmost counties of Scotland, in the charters and documents of the twelfth century.

One version of the adoption of surnames in Scotland makes out that Malcolm Canmore had held a council at Forfar in 1061 and that a rule was then adopted by which surnames taken from territorial possessions were to be assumed by the chief men in the kingdom.[5] A metrical version of this story informs us that, with the Princess Margaret, there came to Scotland:

'Lyndesay, Wallace, Touris and Lovell,
Ramsay, Prestoun, Sandelandis, Bisset, Soulis, Maxwell,
Wardlaw, Giffurd, Maule, Borthwick also,
Fethikran, Creichtoun, all thir and no mo'

Of these, five we are told came 'with Edgar out of Ungary'. Certainly many great Scottish families did originate from these English exiles. The distinguished house of Swinton of Swinton is derived from the Edulfings of Northumbria, independent sovereigns for 200 years before the Conquest.[6] The great family of Drummond, Earls of Perth, 'according to unswerving tradition are of Hungarian origin, Maurice, the first of the family who settled in Scotland, having come from that country with Edgar Atheling and Margaret his sister, afterwards wife of Malcolm III.'[7]

In the the matter of names it is worth noting that while Malcolm III bore a Gaelic nickname, his three sons by Margaret, who all succeeded him, bore English or non-Celtic names—Edgar, Alexander and David. Malcolm and Margaret had in all six sons—Edward, Ethelred and Edmund, besides the three who became kings—and two daughters, Edith and Mary. The latter married Eustace, Count of Boulogne, while Edith, otherwise known as Matilda, married Henry I of England, thus uniting the English with the Norman royal line. The name 'Alexander', Margaret had brought from Hungary. It is a Greek name but it became completely naturalised in Scotland and gave rise to the popular form, 'Sandy.'

Of the fifteen kings between Malcolm III and James I (1406–37), only three bear Celtic names, these being Donald Ban (1093–4) and (1094–7), Duncan II (1094) and Malcolm IV (1153–65). As with the names of the kings, so with those of the bishops did Celtic names give way to English, and later to Norman.

Celtic reaction against the changes brought about by Malcolm and Margaret resulted in Malcolm III being succeeded by his brother, despite the existence of several grown-up sons. One of the marks of change in western Europe in the eleventh and twelfth centuries was the attempt to bring native churches into line with the practice of the Roman Church. There is no doubt that the eagerness with which Rome backed William the Conqueror was due to a desire to get a much firmer control of the English Church. Now in Scotland the same desire manifested itself through the Englishwoman, Margaret. The Celtic churches had differences from the practice of Rome; they kept the beginning of Lent on the Monday following Ash Wednesday, did not take Communion on Easter Day, had a different form of tonsure for their priests, allowed marriage with a deceased brother's wife, and other smaller matters. Roman customs were made to prevail or, as it would have seemed to the Celtic clergy, English customs and forms of worship. Besides these ecclesiastical changes, there was also grumbling among the native magnates about the favouritism shown to strangers who were given places of importance often because they were more able and were familiar with the more advanced governmental system of England.

Malcolm's support of his brother-in-law, Edgar, was not merely nominal, though self-interest had a place in his actions. Not until the English Henry II's time did the counties of Cumberland and Northumberland become properly part of England, previously being claimed by both English and Scots and in dispute between them. The Norman Domesday Book does not include them in its survey.

Malcolm invaded the north of England five times, finally provoking William the Conqueror into a powerful punitive expedition in 1072. William, like another Agricola, advanced with land and sea forces to Abernethy on the Tay, where he confronted Malcolm and there Malcolm did William homage. The occasion was not only a matter of William taking revenge for an invasion of his kingdom. He was the most exacting of men and was well aware that his English predecessors had possessed a supremacy—vague no doubt, but the supremacy of overlord as opposed to vassal—in relation to the other princes of Britain. Consequently, when he had made himself King of all England, he had in the process incorporated Cornwall into England once for all, and compelled the Welsh princes to do him homage while still allowing his barons to invade south Wales. Now he took the same homage from the Scots king. Edgar the Peaceful (died in 975) had been rowed on the Dee by half a dozen vassal kings. William had been crowned according to the form of Edgar's coronation rites and he saw to it that all claims of suzerainty existing in Edgar's reign came to him with Edgar's Crown.[8]

The subject of the feudal supremacy of the English monarch over the Scottish king is even now one to cause high feeling. The claim took many forms but was never, in practice, renounced. It bedevilled Scottish-English relations for hundreds of years. Its importance in clan history is that it is yet another witness to the feudalism which had now reached Scotland.[9] The system is not hard to understand. In theory, the feudal king owned the land and let it out to vassals who sub-let in their turn. Only the King had absolute ownership, a concept quite opposed to the clan principle where the land belongs to the whole clan and cannot be disposed of by the chief. The chief may even be removed by the clan, a revolutionary thought according to feudal ideas.

The feudalism introduced in Malcolm Canmore's time was to be long in conflict with the clan system. Sometimes a feudal lord became, as with the Frazers and the Chisholms, a clan chief, when he and his followers formed a clan. In the later centuries of clan history a measure of feudalism had come into the clan system, so that a chief could be not only head of his clan but, in addition, feudal lord and landlord. In the '45 the chiefs, like 'the gentle Lochiel', were able to call out their clansmen as being their tenants. In other cases a half-and-half arrangement existed which caused immense trouble. A chief of a clan acquired legal rights to land where another clan lived. The rent duty which the clansmen owed to him could easily

C

conflict with the duty to their chief. When, as in the seventeenth century a clan—such as that of the Campbells—grew very powerful, this situation could easily arise.

A new style of court life with more splendour and better manners, came in with Margaret's tenure of the position of queen and co-ruler of the kingdom. Another momentous change was the increasing use of English at Malcolm's court and in southern Scotland. Malcolm himself had learned English and naturally spoke Gaelic and in this tongue he would act as interpreter for his wife in the church councils.

In his last invasion of Northumberland, Malcolm Canmore was killed at Alnwick with his eldest son, Edward. Margaret survived him by only a few days. She was soon canonised and her chapel in Edinburgh Castle remains a hallowed place of national memory. The Celtic reaction did not last long. Four years after Malcolm's death, he was succeeded by his son, Edgar, of whom it has been said '[his] accession and reign of ten years ended the Celtic line in Scotland. Since Donald Ban, no Celt in both lines has sat on the Scottish throne. English and Normans now flocked in and obtained the best of what Edgar and his successors had to give. The long process by which English brewers, soap-boilers and upholsterers sit in the seats of the Macdonnells and Macphersons.'[10]

Under the reign of the third of Malcolm's sons to rule, that of David I, the influx of foreigners became even greater. Many Normans who were dissatisfied with England, or who were younger sons without patrimony, went to Scotland to make their fortunes. A family as Scottish as Haig derived from this source, as do the Barclays, a branch of the Berkeleys of England, whose heiress married an Englishman from Bristol.[11]

In 1138, when David I invaded England and was defeated at the battle of the Standard, his Galloway warriors were the typical half-clad British tribesmen, not so far removed from those who had fought the Romans. They still spoke their Celtic tongue, but a century and a half later the speech of Galloway, as of all southern Scotland, was Scots, a variant of English. The gulf between the Highlander and the folk of the Lowlands had widened so that he was looked on as barbarous, a savage and a foreigner. This despite the fact that, in 1314 at Bannockburn, there were several clans on Bruce's side. But so there were on the side of Edward II. While some clans fought bravely for Bruce, others tried to defeat him, a pattern which was to repeat itself through 450 years right up to Culloden. The Gael was never united.

4 Early Clan Struggles

IT HAS BEEN said with justice that 'the early history of the Macdonalds is the early history of not only the Western Isles but also of the greater part of the Highlands'.[1] Certainly, to understand the facts of clan history it is necessary to know how the races which made up Scotland developed. Maps are the best illustrations of the process. At first, the Picts in their kingdom of Alban controlled Scotland from the borders of Caithness to the line of the Forth and Clyde. When Kenneth MacAlpine combined the monarchies of Picts and Scots, his realm stretched down to the borders of what is now England. At the same time the Norwegians had gained control of the Hebrides and of the west coast of Scotland, part of Argyllshire, Kintyre, Ross and Cromarty. In the course of the next 200 years there emerged the power of Somerled, son of Gillebride, who founded the clan Donald. He headed resistance to the Norwegians and won over large areas from them: the whole of Morvern, Lochaber and the north of Argyll. This was before 1135, for about that year David I of Scotland conquered Arran and Bute, and appears to have conferred these islands upon Somerled. The grant was probably made in the terms of the feudalism with which David I was becoming familiar and he no doubt envisaged Somerled as his vassal. The latter did not take the same view but looked on the territories as his own. In any case, Somerled's position was ambiguous. He had asserted the independence of his people against the Norsemen but he could not defy indefinitely the resources of the Norwegian king. For another hundred years the Norse were to retain control of the western Isles.

Somerled therefore made a marriage with Ragnhildis, daughter of the Norwegian King of the Isles and of Man. By this alliance he secured peace with the Norsemen, but at the same time his relations with the King of Scots were ambivalent. When Somerled had gained Morvern and other territories from the Vikings, they were lands which could hardly be described as Scottish, except retrospectively or in a geographical sense. They were ruled by the Norwegian king and, in conquering them, Somerled won them for himself. As to Arran and Bute, he may well have reasoned that King David would not be able to control these islands. Whatever the explanation, Somerled certainly acted as an independent sovereign. In 1164 he was at war with Malcolm IV, leading an invasion into Renfrewshire where he was killed. Before this conflict Somerled had made a further extension of his powers. The Norse King of Man, Godred, was hated by his subjects, who appealed to Somerled to put forward his son Dougal as King of Man. After a fierce sea battle between Godred (who was Dougal's uncle) and Somerled, the former conceded to Somerled and his sons the rule over the South Isles, while he retained the sovereignty of North Isles and Man. The history of Man is one of intermittent struggle between Norse and Highlander, Scot and English, until in 1405 the island came under the rule of the Stanleys, Earls of Derby.

Somerled was twice married, but the descent of his line eventually came through his two eldest sons by his second marriage. They were Dougall, ancestor of the clan Dougall, MacDougall, living in Argyll and Lorn; and Reginald, from whom came the MacDonalds of Islay, and the Macrories of Bute. This Reginald was styled King of the Isles, Lord of Argyll and Kintyre, and was succeeded by his son, Donald of the Isles, who proclaimed himself King of Man. He had married a daughter of the High Steward of Scotland and was succeeded by his son, Angus Mhor MacDonald, Lord of Inchegal. It was during his time that the Norsemen were defeated by Alexander III at Largs, in Ayrshire, in 1263. In the ensuing Treaty of Perth in 1266, the Western Isles and Man were ceded to the Scottish Crown for a payment of 4,000 marks and a stipulated rental of 100 marks (not paid). The Orkneys and Shetlands remained Norse for another 200 years, but Scotland had otherwise reached her modern boundaries. The accomplishment had come during the rule of her ancient Celtic monarchy. Relations with England had been peaceful for a century 'But the position of the Lord of the Isles remaining till the end of the 15th century in the hands of the descendants and successors of Somerled—Celtic families with a strain of Norse blood—was for long a thorn in the side of the Scottish Kings.'[2]

For 200 years after the Treaty of Perth the Lords of the Isles persistently opposed the Scots kings. The bright exception to this was in the great War of Independence waged by Robert the Bruce against England. As in every succeeding age right up to the '45, the clans were divided in allegiance. The Mac-Dougalls, Lords of Lorn, were related to the Red Comyn, whom Bruce had killed in the church at Dumfries. They were therefore in blood feud against Bruce, and when the latter had first raised his standard as independent King of Scots and had been defeated by the English at Methven he was in great danger from the Lord of Lorn. Bruce had had to take to the heather with his queen, a few faithful lords and ladies, and a small band of followers, not above 300 in all. Suddenly, near the head of the Tay, the MacDougall chief came at Bruce's party. There were about 1,000 Highlanders, lightly armoured men but equipped with the dreaded Lochaber axe and able to move on the rocks with uncommon agility. After a desperate encounter, Bruce succeeded in sending the whole of his party, some of whom were wounded, up a steep narrow path while he in his armour and mounted on his warhorse barred the way. With a savage indifference to their lives, the half-naked clansmen went for Bruce till their bodies mounted in a pile beneath his horse's feet. Even the MacDougall, Bruce's sworn enemy, could not withhold his admiration and compared him to a brilliant champion of Gaelic romance defending his followers from Fingal. At last three Highlanders sprang at Bruce simultaneously; one seized his bridle, another caught him by leg and stirrup, while the third leapt on him, Indian fashion, from behind. He who clasped the bridle had his arm severed by Bruce's sword; the second was thrown down and trampled under the horse's feet; from the third Bruce at last freed himself. With one stroke, Bruce cleft the man's skull but such was his dying tenacity that Bruce could not shake him off except by unclasping his cloak. The brooch thus left behind is a treasured heirloom of the MacDougall chief, and is called the Brooch of Lorn.

If one branch sprung from Somerled's progeny could thus pursue Bruce with hatred, another could offer if anything as fierce an animosity. The elder son of Angus Mhor MacDonald, that is, Alexander, Lord of the Isles, with his seven sons, fought on the English side against Bruce. He was imprisoned by Bruce after the tide of war had turned in Scotland's favour and he and his children disappear from history. As for the Lord of Lorn, Bruce routed his clan near Loch Awe, forced the chief to take refuge in his galley on the loch, and later captured the MacDougall stronghold, Dunstaffnage Castle, near Oban, in Argyllshire.

This by no means ended the line of the Lords of the Isles. A younger brother of Alexander, Angus Og, was a supporter of Bruce, again following the pattern of clan division with members of the same blood group on opposing sides. Angus Og, with the bulk of the Islesmen, was at Bannockburn in 1314, along with other clansmen on Bruce's side. Bravely and well the Macdonalds fought on the right wing, thus establishing a precedent which they were to claim with dire results over 400 years later at Culloden.

It is interesting to reflect that had the whole MacDonald clan fought against Bruce, they could all have been dispossessed, or at least the chiefs could have been driven out, as was Angus Og's brother. In that event all the subsequent trouble with the Lords of the Isles would have been avoided. The act of loyalty to the King of Scots which brought Angus Og to Bannockburn led to the retention of the family possessions, though hardly again were the Lords of the Isles to behave loyally. In this disloyalty, the Highland chiefs must not be blamed as if they alone could be guilty of treachery to Scotland. As all Scottish historians agree, there was always a party or clique among the nobles ready to side with England. Sir James Douglas was Bruce's nearest friend and the one to whom he confided his heart after his death, to be taken to the Holy Land. Douglas was killed in Spain in the attempt, and his life of chivalry, romance and hard fighting has given a glow of romance to the Douglas name. 'For Douglasses were heroes every age.' Brave enough certainly, but after Sir James's time almost uniformly disloyal to the Scots Crown. Even the heir of Bruce's blood, David II, was willing to pass the crown to an English prince, a course in which the Douglas agreed with him. It is a Scotsman who comments on the transaction: 'The son of the Bruce, the nephew of the good Lord James are here found united in an attempt to set an Englishman on the Stone of Destiny.'[3] It was the faith of the common people and their refusal to put out the fire of freedom which had been lighted at Bannockburn that kept Scotland independent.

If, then, in medieval times this tendency to change sides was characteristic of some of Scotland's greatest men, it is not surprising that the Lords of the Isles should have relapsed from their brief loyalty into their more usual state of defiance of the Crown.

John, son of Angus Og, is described as resuming the style of an independent sovereign, and he forsook Bruce's heir, David II, in favour of Edward Balliol (son of the John Balliol whom Edward I of England had decided should be King of Scotland in 1292). Edward Balliol led a small force to Scotland in 1332 and overthrew the Scots army at Dupplin, in Perthshire. Balliol was crowned at Scone on 24 September 1332 but went to England on 16 December of the same year, never having reigned and practically surrendering his rights to the English Edward III.

The Lord of the Isles had been on Balliol's side and when David II came back from France, where he had gone to escape Balliol, it would have been quite usual for the Crown to have declared the territories of John forfeit. There were always two difficulties in the forfeiture of a great Scottish lord. First, the forfeiture had to be carried out, and this was difficult in the Lowlands or on the Borders in medieval times, and even more hazardous in the Highlands. And, secondly, when forfeiture did take place, as with the Black Douglas line, great estates were taken by the Crown but not kept for long, as the Crown had not the administrative means to retain them. During the reigns of most of the Scots kings from Bruce onward, and particularly with the Stuarts from James I, there were many trials for high treason, with loss of heads and lands. One great family went down but soon the forfeited lands were granted to another. There were also numerous intermarriages between the leading families, so that the disfavoured not infrequently won their way back to power and position. The MacDougalls suffered badly after Bruce's victory, but in the reign of David II the MacDougall chief managed to marry a grand-daughter of King Robert Bruce and in this way had his land restored.

It was much the same with the Lords of the Isles after Edward Balliol's failure. David II had to consider how many enemies he could afford to make, especially if it were one whose clansmen could command part of the western coast and islands. In 1344 he therefore took back into his peace both John, Lord of the Isles, and Ranald, chief of the Macrories of Bute, whose father had been forfeited by David's father. The list of the possessions restored shows the vast influence and power possessed by the MacDonald chiefs. To the Lord of the Isles went the islands of Islay, Jura, Gigha, Scarba, Colonsay, Mull, Coll, Tiree and Lewis, plus the large mainland areas of Morvern, Argyllshire, Lochaber, Inverness-shire, Duror and Glencoe. The chief of the Macrories, Ranald, got back Uist, Barra, Eigg and Rum. Another kinsman of the Lord of the Isles, Angust MacIan, got Ardnamurhan and founded the clan MacIan of Ardnamurchan. Considering that, before the '45, even British government forces could not fully control these wild outer regions, one can imagine how impossible the task was in the fourteenth century. The Scots king had to endure what he could not alter.

From John, Lord of the Isles, came many branches of the Macdonald clans which are with us today. John was married twice. By his first marriage he was the ancestor of the Mac-Donalds of Clanranald in North and South Uist, Rum and Eigg, also of the MacDonalds, or MacDonnells, of Glengarry. His second marriage was to the Princess Margaret, daughter of King Robert II, the Steward, and the first of the Stuart kings. By his second wife he had Donald, his successor as Lord of the Isles, and other sons who were the ancestors of the Earls of Antrim, the MacDonalds of Keppoch and the MacDonalds of Cnocandruith. John, Lord of the Isles, died in 1387, having used the principle of tanistry to appoint his successor. By this device the ruling chief could nominate the member of his family who was to succeed him, and who was then known as his tanist, or tanistair.

The next Lord of the Isles was Donald MacDonald, and his connections by marriage had an important influence on the relations between Celt and Saxon and to the great battle of the 'red Harlaw' in 1411. Donald's wife was Mary, or Margaret Leslie, the only daughter of the Countess of Ross by her husband, Sir Andrew Leslie. Margaret's brother was Alexander, who became Earl of Ross and married Isabel, daughter of the Regent, the Duke of Albany, who governed Scotland in the absence of the boy king, James I, detained in England under conditions amounting almost to captivity. Alexander's and Isabel's only child was Euphemia, and by forcing her to enter a convent and renounce her rights to the earldom, Albany hoped to keep the earldom in his own family, since Euphemia had made it over to his heirs male.

Donald MacDonald then asserted a claim to the earldom in right of his wife and prepared to make good his title by force of arms. He gathered a host which was huge by Highland standards, as many as 20,000 men according to some estimates. At Ardtornish Castle on the Sound of Mull, the clans gathered in support of Donald's claim, perhaps in response to the fiery cross. They included the Macleans of Mull, the Macleods of Skye, the Camerons of Lochaber, the Clan Chattan (a huge collection of tribes), and the numerous branches of the MacDonalds. Had Prince Charles been able to muster such a host he might have regained his father's kingdom. But the curse of disunity which attended the clans in all their history once again prevailed. At Dingwall, the Highland army met another force from the north, the tribes from Caithness and Sutherland, under Angus Mackay. They were defeated and the Lord of the Isles marched on with his tribal army.

> ... Donald came branking down the brae
> Wi' twenty thousand men
> Their tartans they were waving wide
> Their glaives were glancing clear
> The pibrochs rung frae side to side
> Would deafen ye to hear.[4]

As they approached Aberdeen, they were met at Harlaw by the Earl of Mar with a small force of knights, Lowland gentry and some of the city burgesses. There followed a grim battle lasting until nightfall, a struggle bloody enough to earn for it the title in folk memory of 'red Harlaw'. The mail-clad Lowlanders could ride almost at will among the Highlanders until their horses were dirked or shot by arrows, for the clansmen were good archers. The losses on the Lowland side were heavy in leaders and among the gentry, though not as great as those of the Highlanders. The battle was indecisive though Aberdeen was saved from sack and the Highland Host retreated. It was heavy with plunder, a fact of great importance in a Highland army. Donald had gained much booty from the northern coastal plain and unless he had promised his followers huge spoils from Aberdeen and the south, they would never have marched across the country from west to east.

The battle of Harlaw is often described as the last trial of supremacy between Saxon and Gael, but this is incorrect. Exactly when supremacy passed to the Saxon, or English, element is not easy to determine but the complete triumph of the Southron, or Sassenach, did not come until Culloden. Donald's raid was one of many in clan history, with the added incentive that he aspired to an earldom carrying with it larger territories in the north. In addition, he was in the pay of Henry IV of England from 1408, a factor which was to be recurrent in Highland affairs throughout the history of the Lords. In the year following the battle of Harlaw, the Duke of Albany marched to Dingwall and there received the submission of Donald.

When Donald died in 1420 he left two sons, Alexander, who succeeded him, and Angus, later Bishop of the Isles. In 1424, James I took possession of his kingdom, determined to restore order within it, to punish those who had caused the death of his elder brother, the Duke of Rothesay, and to make the Highlands as orderly as he hoped the Lowlands would be. In dealing with the Highland chiefs, James called them to a parliament at Inverness in 1427 and we can form a good conception of life in the Highlands at that time by studying the record of this assembly. One of the Lord Alexander's uncles, John Mhor, was killed by another of the delegates, James Campbell, and other tribal feuds existed among those summoned. The King took no half measures but laid hold of the chiefs and put most of them in prison. This was the customary way of dealing with these wild men, who had to be lured into a meeting with the King. The royal attitude towards them seems to have been based on the alleged principle of the Crusaders, 'no faith with infidels'. Time and again during the Stuart monarchy in Scotland a Highland chief was persuaded that the King merely wanted to talk with him, but as soon as he was in the King's power he was seized and imprisoned, and lucky to save his life. In Alexander's case, he was imprisoned for a time and when released in 1429 showed his real feelings by burning Inverness. King James then brought an army against him and defeated him in Lochaber. After an abject submission at Holyrood in his shirt and drawers, he was imprisoned in the Douglas stronghold, Tantallon Castle, overlooking the North Sea, almost as far from his home as Scotland's boundaries would allow. The earldom of Ross was confirmed to him and he appears to have remained fairly quiet until his death in 1449.

In the meantime it may be noted that the Clan Chattan had deserted the Lords of the Isles, as had also Clan Cameron, but this did not mean that they were particularly law-abiding. Clan Chattan in 1430 succeeded in burning a church with some of Clan Cameron inside.

None of King James's forceful actions pacified the Highlands for long. Donald Balloch, son of the murdered John Mhor, raised a revolt and overthrew the royal army at Inverlochy. He withdrew to Ireland, whence someone's head was sent to the King as that of Donald Balloch, though in fact he did not die until 1476.

The next Lord of the Isles, John, who was also Earl of Ross, brought about the ruin of his family by over-reaching himself in acting as an independent sovereign and treating directly with Edward IV of England. This Yorkist monarch, having secured control of England and her dominions, had no intention of intervening in the affairs of Scotland or of France. He did once take an army to France, but withdrew on receiving a substantial payment from Louis XI and what amounted to a yearly pension. With Scotland, he was content to foment trouble by means of the MacDonalds, and the treaty he made in 1461 with the Lord of the Isles allowed for the dismemberment of Scotland between himself, MacDonald and the Earl of Douglas. The result was rebellion in the north and on the Scottish border.

On discovery of the facts, there could be no quarter for what was unquestionably high treason, and by the concurring judgement of his peers—Argyll, Crawford, Atholl and Huntley—John, Lord of the Isles, had in 1476 to forfeit the earldom of Ross, together with his lands in Inverness, Nairn, Knapdale and Kintyre. The King, James III, granted to him his title of Lord of the Isles as a dignity in the peerage of Scotland and he was left with his ancestral lands. These possessions, however, were not enough for his son Angus (assassinated at Inverness in 1490), still less for his grandson, Donald Dubh who, after spending much time in prison, escaped to Ireland and died at Drogheda, 'leaving a son of whom no more is heard' (*Burke's Peerage*, MacDonald).

Donald Dubh held himself out as Lord of the Isles and as being able to make treaties on equal terms with Henry VIII. Thus, as late as 1545 there was still the faint threat of menace from the ancient line of the MacDonald sub-kings. John, the great-grandfather of Donald Dubh and the last true Lord of the Isles, died in 1503, and from that date until 1660 the Clan Donald was treated as chiefless. The subsequent history of the chiefship is common form to the innumerable clan history books and to the genealogy of Lord MacDonald of Slate, Co Antrim in Ireland, chief of the name and arms of MacDonald.

After the forfeiture, the title of Lord of the Isles was annexed to the style of the heir to the Scottish throne. As such, it passed to the heir to both England and Scotland, so that the Prince of Wales has among his Welsh and English titles several which recall the old Scottish monarchy: Duke of Rothesay, Earl of Carrick and Baron of Renfrew in the Peerage of Scotland, Lord of the Isles and Great Steward of Scotland. Thus it is that the heir to the British throne has in his style a faint reminiscence of long-past struggles, when the full sovereignty of the King of Scots was still in dispute.

Although the MacDonalds were the largest clan in the Highlands, and by reason of their chief the most important in medieval Scotland, they were not the only clans to give trouble to the Scottish government. The first two Stuart kings—Robert II and Robert III—were weak rulers and it was not remarkable that under them there should be difficulties with the Highlanders. One of the causes of trouble lay in the economic stresses of life in the Highlands. Cattle-rearing and fishing, with the raising of scanty crops in the small areas of the glens available for cultivation, were the only natural resources of the clansmen, apart from hunting deer and trapping smaller prey, such as the hare. After a hard winter or a bad harvest, with perhaps an unusually large increase in the population, there was the danger of real hunger, and it was natural that strong, able-bodied men with abundant weapons at hand, should look to the Lowlands where it seemed that food in plenty as well as valuable booty was to be found. Such raids by the Highlanders upon their Lowland neighbours did not cease entirely until after the '45, despite the raising from 1729 onward of independent companies with the object of preventing cattle raids. The situation was not dissimilar to that which prevailed on the North-West Frontier of British India, and the independent companies may not unreasonably be likened to the various frontier forces raised by the British from among the very tribesmen who were wont to raid across the frontier.

The well-known expression, the Highland Line, refers to the frontier, or dividing line between the Lowlanders' territory and that occupied by the clans. It was an imaginary line which stretched diagonally across Scotland from the Firth of Clyde up to the Firth of Tay. It separated the Gaelic speakers from those who spoke a dialect of English, and the speaking of English was universal throughout the Lowlands after the War of Independence in the early thirteenth century. After the establishment of the Stuart monarchy it would be unusual for a Scots king to know Gaelic and James IV's mastery of the language was one of the many accomplishments of that versatile monarch. The Highland Line traversed a large area south of the Grampian range, always on the edge of mountainous country and accessible only by passes which were easily defended.

The country most exposed to Highland raids was obviously that nearest to the mountains, and only on great occasions did a chief gather men from distant areas and lead them into Lowland territory. On the whole the clansmen did not fight for love of war, or for glory, but for economic reasons or because of blood feuds. Proof of this is seen in the difficulty which even the most renowned leaders had in keeping their Highland army together, a feat that neither Montrose nor Bonnie Prince Charlie were able to achieve. The tendency was for the Highland Host to fight a quick action, get as much spoil as possible and then go home to the glens to enjoy it. Although in the '45 a total of some 8,000 clansmen were out for Prince Charles, his army did not number as many in any of the three battles which he fought or in his march to Derby.

While the clans bordering on the Lowlands could gain supplies from their raids, those who dwelt at a distance were less favourably placed and so were apt to engage in inter-tribal struggles for land and influence, often accentuated by occasional blood feuds such as the famous instance between Bruce and the MacDougalls. On the forfeiture of a clan there was always a scramble for the available land, as when the Mackenzies in Ross and Cromarty benefited from the fall of the Lords of the Isles. In later clan history, from about 1500 onwards, the Campbells took the place of the Macdonalds as the most powerful clan, and as will be seen, greatly increased their own holdings at the expense of those clans who were unlucky in their rebellions against government.

The greater clans had many branches or septs, as was particularly the case with the MacDonalds. Apart, however, from the cadet branches connected by blood with the chief of the clan, there were ten tribes which were vassals of the great clan. The relationship was fairly loose and not by any means like the strict feudal nexus in England or southern Scotland. 'Other clans, Macleods, Macleans, Mcneills, Clan Chattan and Cameron, and numerous septs of lesser note, had a long-standing connection with the Lords of the Isles.'[5] Here was a confederacy of clans, not necessarily connected by blood, and in the straitened circumstances of the Highlands, any two such associations of clans could keep the Highlands disturbed by their battles for supremacy.

In the reign of Robert III (1390–1406) a violent commotion did upset the Highlands. As so often happened with a weak king or a monarch in his minority, the appointed guardians of the peace abused their position and sided with the makers of disorder. The King's younger brother, Alexander, Earl of Buchan, had been appointed Justiciary in the northern Lowlands. He has gone down in history by the picturesque title of the 'Wolf of Badenoch'[6] (eastern Inverness-shire), and it is clear from the record of events under his jurisdiction that he did not in any way restrain the caterans, the term applied pejoratively by Lowlanders to the Highland freebooters. In Scots Gaelic the word meant 'peasantry' and in Irish Gaelic 'a band of soldiers', but to the caterans' victims they appeared only as thieving and murderous. The Wolf of Badenoch was removed from the Justiciarship in 1389 but this made for little or no improvement; the Wolf burnt down Elgin Cathedral in 1390. One of his bastards, Alexander, after the murder of the Countess of Mar's husband, married her by force and became Earl of Mar. By 1411 he had become the leader of the gentry at Harlaw.

Another bastard of the Wolf, Duncan, led the caterans into the Braes of Angus and killed the county sheriff along with many others. An incident characteristic of the toughness of the Highlanders is recorded of this fight. 'A Highlander, speared by David Lindsay, writhed up the spear shaft and cut through the knight's boot and stirrup leather to the bone and died in that stroke'.[7]

In view of such disorders it was almost to be expected that rival associations of clans should fight with each other, and one such disturbance which came to the attention of the Scottish Crown in 1395–6 occurred between two combinations of clans. Such is the paucity of exact record about clan history, reflected in the uncertain genealogy of their chiefs, that the identity of the two federations is not exactly known. 'The names, as we have them in Wyntoun, are, "Clanwhewyl" and "Claninchya" the latter probably not correctly transcribed. In the *Scoti-Chronicon* they are "Clanquhele" and "Clankay". Hector Boece writes "Clanchattan" and "Clankay", in which he is followed by Leslie: while Buchan disdains to disfigure his page with their Gaelic designations at all, and merely describes them as two powerful races in the wild and lawless region beyond the Grampians. Out of this jumble what Sassenach can pretend *dare lucem*? The name "Clanwheill" appears as late as 1594 in an Act of James VI. Is it possible that it may be, after all, a mere corruption of Clan Lochiel?'[8]

Thus Sir Walter Scott, to whose opinion can be added that of Andrew Lang that the combatants were Clan Chattan and the Camerons. George Eyre Todd[9] more or less concurs in this, joining up the combat of 1396 at Perth with a defeat of Clan Chattan by the Camerons because of the defection of the Macphersons from Clan Chattan. The Macphersons were induced to attack the Camerons by an aspersion on their bravery made by Mackintosh, Chief of Clan Chattan. 'One of the results of this encounter remains among the most famous episodes in Scottish history.'[9]

The episode was the famous fight of thirty champions on either side which took place in 1396 on the North Inch, a public meadow, plain, or park at Perth. It is tempting to think that this conflict was brought about as the result of some deep, if rather diabolical, thinking on the part of the King's Council. The Highlands were in turmoil and, at Perth, the consequences of clan unrest were only too easily felt. Why not, then, get thirty a side of the bravest warriors and let them kill off each other, thus depriving both confederations of their natural leaders and bringing peace for a time to the clan areas? It may have been so, but the idea of such a combat was very much in accord with the spirit of the age, and the rough chivalry of similar encounters. To quote only three examples: before Bannockburn, the only important English stronghold in Scotland was Stirling Castle, and when the English governor agreed with Robert the Bruce to surrender if he were not relieved in a year and a day, he faithfully kept his word. Again, in the reign of Edward III, there was the famous combat of the Thirty in Brittany, when thirty English and allied knights fought thirty French, just for the love of fighting. In 1400, the Duke of Rothesay issued a challenge to Henry IV to settle Scottish–English differences in an engagement with so many knights on either side.

Perhaps it was the same motivation which led to the combat at the North Inch, though the callous indifference shown to the deaths of sixty men is certainly more in keeping with the policy of the Scots kings towards their Highland subjects. At this combat on the North Inch an immense concourse of people were present, with King Robert III and his principal nobles. The two bodies of clansmen fought bloodily and the Clan Chattan were the winners, though the survivors on their side were all badly wounded. Of the other party to the dispute, the Camerons, it is traditionally asserted that only one survived

D

and that he did so by fleeing from the lists and swimming across the Tay. Probably most readers of Scott have had their outlook on the matter very much coloured by his account of the matter in *The Fair Maid of Perth*. He, to his own satisfaction, ended the story with a result in accordance with the allegedly deep-laid plot of the King's Council. 'The consequence of their defeat [ie, of 'Clan Quhele'] was the dissolution of their confederacy. The clans of which it consisted are now only matter of conjecture to the antiquary, for after this eventful contest, they never assembled under the same banner. The Clan Chattan, on the other hand, continued to increase and flourish, and the best families of the Northern Highlands boast their descent from the race of the Cat-a-Mountain.'[10] The last allusion is to the badge of Clan Chattan, a wild cat with the motto 'Touch not the cat bot a glove' (ie, without a glove).

Clan Chattan was an ancient federation of clans, rather resembling the League of the Six Nations in Canada in which the Iroquois were the leading tribe. Clan Chattan included the Mackintoshes, Davidsons, Macphersons, Macgillivrays, Macbeans and Farquharsons. Among these clans, one had to provide the head, or Captain of Clan Chattan, and dispute as to this was made between Mackintosh and MacPherson. The first authentic chief is said to have been Gillechattan Mor, and from him descended the 6th Chief Dougall Dall, whose daughter and only child, Eva, married Angus, the 6th Chief of Mackintosh. The MacPherson chief also claimed the headship of the Clan Chattan, but in 1672 the Lord Lyon decided in favour of Mackintosh because his predecessor had married the heretrix of the Clan Chattan, so ending a feud which had lasted for 200 years. In 1938 the 28th Mackintosh of Mackintosh died without male issue. He had nominated his tanist, or successor, as Chief of Clan Mackintosh but not of Clan Chattan, and the headship of the latter went in 1947 to Duncan Alexander Eliot Mackintosh of Mackintosh-Torcastle, recognised by the Lord Lyon as 31st Chief of Clan Chattan.

The meaning of Clan Chattan is sometimes given as the clan of the cats, but more likely is the explanation, 'Servants of St Chattan', meaning that Gillechattan was the bailie, or temporal custodian, of the abbey lands of Ardchattan. The first chief lived in the reign of Malcolm III (1058–63).[11]

With the death of the last Lord of the Isles in 1503, only another century remains before the union of the Crowns of England and Scotland gave to the Scots king a great accession of power. When Scotland was a separate state it was not only the country behind the Highland Line which was a centre of unrest. There were also frequent disturbances in the Border country between England and Scotland. The Scottish people who lived on or near the Borders are often referred to as clans, but they were really families of the same name, like the Elliots, Armstrongs, Johnstons and Maxwells. They differed from the Highlanders in race, language, dress, style of weapons, use of horses, and in almost every other respect. The fact that they are sometimes included as clans may derive from the frequency with which they are bracketed with the Highlanders in Acts of the Scots Parliament.

In the sixteenth century three Acts of Parliament were passed in the short period from 1587 to 1597.[12] The first of these, in 1587, was called an Act for Quietening the Borders, Highlands and Isles. It gives the names of clans with captains, chiefs and chieftains. In 1594, an Act for the punishment of theft and other crimes gave a list of clans and surnames in the Highlands and Isles, also list of broken men. These last were persons such as the remnants of Scott's Clan Quhele. Their clan had disintegrated and they had to get in somewhere, if only for the sake of their daily bread, so when a chief proved willing to adopt them, they took his surname.

The third Act, in 1597, had for its purpose, 'That the inhabitants of Isles and Highlands show their holding'. This was a demand that 'sheepskin' charters, ie, documents, should be produced just as they would be in the Lowlands or in England. From this period, the end of the sixteenth century onwards, the clan system was in process of erosion, though 150 years were to go by before its fall. The demand for deeds, charters and documentary proof aided some few of the chiefs, such as the Dukes of Argyll, but it introduced into Highland society conceptions incompatible with the clan system and also with feudal ideas which had to some extent been worked into the clan life. From now on there began to be written histories of the leading Highland families in which pretensions were asserted and even spurious charters inserted. From these manuscripts were compiled histories of clans which form the basis of most peerage and baronetage accounts, and also of the 'Enquiry into the Genealogy and Present State of the Ancient Scottish Surnames, with the Origin and Descent of the Highland Clans and Family of Buchanan', by William Buchanan of Auchmar, published in 1723.

The culture of the Highlands was not stationary. It underwent many changes, and saw the use of very different weapons. The fighters on the North Inch used heavy, long, two-handed swords; by the seventeenth century these had given way to the basket-hilted broadsword, further reference to which is made in the next chapter.

The earlier reference to broken men poses the question how far a clan was allied by blood to the chief. In all probability, only a minority were in each clan. The origin of some clans is not Celtic, Gunn being Norse, and Fraser and Chisholm Normans from the Border. The Grahams also came from the Border and may have been Norman in origin. In these and other cases a feudal lord and his following became clansfolk in a short time, or at least their descendants soon did. In other words, once having settled in clan territory these newcomers assumed control and conformed to existing customs. They must, therefore, have gathered in many people who were not of their blood but who became their clan 'children' and adopted their name. As ages passed and clans rose and fell, the remnants of defeated clans had to look out for fresh chiefs. It is often said that comparatively pure clan blood is to be found in the MacGregors. They were forbidden to use their surname for close on 200 years, yet in 1795 no less than 826 persons of the name came forward to discard the clan surnames by which they and their forbears had been known and to resume their patronymic.

5 Highland Way of Life and Culture

ONE OF THE most distinguishing features of the Highlands is, in most people's minds, the peculiar dress associated with the clans. Highland dress has a long history of development and the subject has now been very carefully studied by historians; the references in literature and other documents have been analysed; delineations of Highland or alleged Highland dress (perhaps it would be better to say of Scottish dress) on monuments, in paintings and in book or manuscript illustrations have all been examined and can be seen in many works dealing with clan tartans.[1]

The connection between the Scottish Highlands and Ireland was, as we have seen, close for many ages, and though it was severed from 1600 following the English conquest of Ireland at the end of Elizabeth I's reign, seventeenth-century writers frequently continued to refer to Gaelic as Irish (Erse). The English connection with Ireland from 1169 had not meant any real colonisation of Ireland. The great Anglo-Norman lords who conquered and divided the country were absorbed by the Irish and became themselves leaders in rebellion against England. Under the Tudors there was almost continuous trouble in Ireland, and on several occasions pretenders to the English throne and rebels against it necessitated the despatch of English armies to Ireland. After Mountjoy's defeat of the rebels at Kinsale there were rebellions and commotions but, right up to the Easter Rising of 1916, such disturbances were quickly suppressed. The English drastically affected Ireland and many Irish customs had to be abandoned, among them the distinctive Irish dress, whose disappearance had considerable repercussions on their Highland kinsfolk.

In passing, it may be recalled that the Scots who gave their name to ancient Alban were an Irish tribe. Also that those in trouble in Scotland generally sought refuge in Ireland. Edward Bruce, King Robert the Bruce's brother, even contemplated a repetition in Ireland of his brother's success in Scotland. He was accepted by some of the Irish as King of Ireland, but was soon afterwards defeated and killed at Dundalk.

The ancient Irish dress which was common to the Highlanders points to an original of unknown antiquity, which may go back as far as ancient Gaul or to the costumes of the Celtic peoples in western Europe before Christ. Two styles of dress are found in old Ireland, a long close-fitting smock called the *léine*, with an outer mantle, the *brat*, which was apparently worn by the wealthier inhabitants, and a dress in the form of a jacket and trews, either long or short, as shown in the famous Book of Kells. There was also a kind of loin cloth but this must have been, in view of the Irish climate, a very auxiliary garment. The reasonable presumption is that two races existed in pre-historic Ireland, and that the wearers of the *léine* and *brat* were of the conquerors. Trews, of course, mean breeches but when modern regiments are said to 'wear the trews', the reference is not to the old form of dress but to tartan-pattern trousers.

Saffron, yellow, was the colour of the garments of the upper classes in Ireland in pre-Conquest days, saffron being a dye made from the dried stigmas of the autumn crocus. The name of Croydon in Surrey, England, is supposed to mean the saffron valley, either because of the prevalence of crocuses there, or because of their cultivation as a dye. Cultivation of the crocus was certainly the reason for the name of Saffron Walden, in Essex, where production of the dye continued until as late as 1768. In Ireland, Castle Saffron in County Cork is said to derive its name from the quantity of crocuses which were formerly grown there. The word 'saffron' is from the Arabic but the dye was known to the Greeks as 'krokos', whence the Latin *crocus* and the Irish *cróch*. The colour is definitely bright yellow and there is no evidence to support its application to the brown shade now frequently described as saffron.[2]

Such, then, was the Irish national dress against which laws were passed during the Tudor period. Many enactments were also made against English people who lived in the Pale (the area around Dublin) marrying Irish husbands or wives. As regards the sumptuary laws, there was an Act of 28 Henry VIII XV which forbade the use of the Irish national dress after 1 May 1539. Another Act passed in Dublin in 1541 limited the amount of linen cloth to be used in shirts.

As for the use of tartan in Ireland, the best authorities do not consider there is any evidence of this in the sixteenth century, nor do they think that an Irish kilt existed. One of them—H. J. McClintock, the learned author of *Old Irish and Highland Dress*—wrote:

> I think that, on investigation the theory (ie, of an Irish kilt) will be found to be a comparatively modern one and to have originated with O'Curry in the middle of the 19th century, strengthened by the belief then prevalent in the great antiquity of the Highland kilt, and by the assumption that what was worn in ancient times by the Scottish Gaels must have been also worn by their fellow Celts in Ireland . . . and it is enough to say here that there is no evidence to show that the Highland kilt was evolved till long after the Irish national dress had gone out of use. It could not therefore have had anything to do with any Irish kilt real or supposed [op cit, p 121].

It is sometimes suggested that a kilt-like garment is shown on some Irish effigies, eg, the O'Cahan tomb at Dungiven, Co Londonderry, or the Burke effigy at Glinck (Ouglinsk), Co Galway, where the figures are sculptured in the 'haqueton' or 'acton', the Irish cotún, a garment in the form of a long coat reaching below the knees. It was quilted vertically so that it did often resemble a kilt, or rather the edge of a pleated kilt. 'It was, of course, not a kilt at all; nor, except in a superficial way and that only when its upper part is hidden, is it the least like one.' (McClintock, op cit, p 69.) The same writer, in his *Old Highland Dress and Tartans* (1949), points out that very little is ascertainable about Highland costume before the sixteenth century. He considered, however, that the saffron shirt or tunic was the garb of the Highlanders. Another modern writer, R. M. D. Grange, in *A Short History of the Highland Dress* (1966), quotes from Robert Lindsay of Pitscottie (who wrote in the sixteenth century): 'They [ie, the Redshanks, or wild Scots] be clothed in one mantle with one shirt saffroned after the Irish manner, going bare-legged to the knee' (op cit, p 26).

Then again, in the same work, there is a quotation from Nicholay d'Arfeville, under the date 1583:

> Those who inhabit Scotland in the south of the Grampian Mountains are tolerably civilized and orderly and speak the English language, but those who inhabit the North are more rude, homely and unruly and for this reason are called 'Wild'. They wear like the Irish a large and full shirt, coloured with saffron and over this a garment hanging to the knee of coarse wool, after the fashion of a cassock. They go bareheaded and let their hair grow very long, and wear neither hose nor shoes except some who have boots made in an old-fashioned way which come as high as their knees.

The term 'Redshanks' was applied to the Highlanders by both themselves and their enemies. A Highland priest who wrote to Henry VIII in 1542–3 signed himself, 'Clerk and Redshank', and explained that the name arose from the Highland custom of going barefooted and barelegged, and from the Highlanders' great ability to endure cold and hardship.

Pictorial evidence confirms the above views. A Low Country artist, Lucas de Heere, who lived as an exile in England from 1567 to 1577, may never have been in Scotland, but in drawing a Scottish Highlander he worked from models, as he did with his Irish subjects. He has left us a representation of a Highlander armed with a large claymore and with a dagger fastened to his belt, and dressed in a tartan or chequered jacket, with a short pleated skirt and very short trews of white material, much like modern football shorts. Apart from these he is barelegged, but has brogues on his feet and a mantle, or plaid, of light-coloured unpatterned cloth thrown over his shoulders. Except that the knees are bare, the costume bears no resemblance to the traditional picture of the Highlander over the last 250 years.

> With the disappearance of the saffron shirt or tunic the Highland costume necessarily underwent a change, and the plaid became more than ever a necessary part of the dress for covering the body below the waist. When so used it was worn with a belt round to keep it in position, thus giving rise to the belted plaid. [McClintock, op cit, p 18.)

The supply of linen from Ireland was cut off after the English Conquest in 1600, and the Irish dress being proscribed, the Highlanders were likewise affected. While the saffron tunic was the wear of the Scottish Highlanders up to the sixteenth century, from the beginning of the seventeenth they used the belted plaid. This was a voluminous garment which could be draped suitably on the person of the wearer so as not to incommode him while walking, and was also sufficient cover during cold or wet weather, or at night. Detailed descriptions are given as to the way in which it was put on. The wearer would arrange it on the ground and when he had got it to his satisfaction he would lie down and fold it round him until completely adjusted. The dimensions of the plaid are given as two yards in width by four or six in length, or about five feet wide, 'made of two single widths of about 30 inches sewn together and usually from 12 to 18 feet in length' (McClintock, p 19).

> In dressing, this was carefully plaited in the middle of a breadth suitable to the size of the wearer, and sufficient to extend from one side around his back to the other, leaving as much at each end as would cover the front of the body overlapping each other. The plaid being thus prepared was firmly bound around the loins with a leathern belt, in such manner that the lower side fell down to the middle of the knee joint, and then, while there were the foldings behind, the cloth was double before. The upper part was then fastened on the left shoulder with a large brooch or pin, so as to display to the most advantage the tastefulness of the arrangement, the two ends being suffered to hang down, but that on the right side which was necessarily the longest was more usually tucked under the belt. [*The Scottish Gael*, James Logan, 1833, p 167.]

In the Low Country it was called the belted plaid, 'to distinguish it from the more usual way in which it was worn by the inhabitants, who merely wrapped it over the left shoulder having small clothes under it' (*ibidem*).

It is not difficult to see the development of the plaid costume from the former Irish dress. A map of Scotland prepared by John Speed (1552–1629) shows a Scots man and a Scots woman clad like their counterparts in England in the reign of Elizabeth I, but of a Highland man half-naked in a tartan garment rather like a midi-length skirt and a Highland woman in a more voluminous version of the same. Again, in a French book called *Receuil de la Diversité des Habits*, which was published in Paris in 1562, we are treated to a representation of a Highland chief—*le capitaine sauvage*; and a woman—*la sauvage d'Écosse*. The chief wears very strange clothes indeed, knees bare it is true but otherwise bearing no resemblance to the chiefs portrayed by Raeburn. The woman is shown enveloped in a huge garment, perhaps her only dress!

With regard to tartan, the arrangement of simple patterns

has probably been widespread among nations, but not in the elaborate form of the present-day clan tartans. Originally, the word meant a light woollen material of any colour, and is derived through the French *tiretaine* from the Spanish *tiritana*. In Gaelic the word *breacan* = tartan cloth, as applied to a blanket, like the voluminous garments of Irish and Highlanders pre-1600. It did not mean what is now called in English a plaid; the word may, says one authority, have been borrowed as no true Gaelic word ever begins with the letter 'p'. As to the origin of the plaid, we know nothing, though it was in use by 1578. The tartan was easy to weave, and such cloths were probably worn by the Celts of old Gaul. Hence the expression in reference to Highlanders as being clad in the 'garb of old Gaul'. There is an alternative explanation. The garb of old Gaul is the name of a song, with words by Lt-General Sir Henry Erskine, Bart, and the tune by Major Reid. One modern Scottish writer[3] states that Gaul and Gael are merely supposed to be the same, this being a piece of typical Scottish mythology, as is also the idea that the ancient Caledonians who fought the Romans were ancestors of the Scots who came to the country long after.

To continue with the terms in Highland dress: trews are simply long hose. The trews used by regiments now are tight-fitting tartan trousers (see above). Tartan is said by some writers to have been first mentioned or recorded in Scotland in 1440, by others that the earliest record is in the Lord High Treasurer's accounts for 1538. James V then had a Highland suit made, consisting of coat, trews and shirt, no mention being made of plaid or kilt. Coming now to the kilt, this word is English from Danish (it is allied to 'quilt') and means something girded or tucked up. It is an exact translation of the Gaelic *filleadh*, and was originally applied to the *filleadh mor*, meaning belted plaid or great *filleadh*; in modern usage it is restricted to *filleadh beg* or *philabeg*. The belted plaid would more properly be called the great kilt, and the philabeg the little kilt.

The latter is, or can be worn separately without the belted plaid. It was the custom of the Highlanders when in battle to throw off the belted plaid before they charged so that it did not hamper their movements. This was all very well when they were going into a fierce combat and likely to emerge victorious, but if by any chance they had to retreat and were swept past their plaids, they would have lost most of their clothes and be exposed to the elements. This actually happened to part of the Earl of Mar's force at Sheriffmuir in 1715, when the men probably had to return home to get fresh clothing.

The saffron tunic, then, was the Highland dress in the sixteenth century, with the belted plaid coming in and forming the standard dress in the seventeenth century. When did the separate kilt or philabeg begin to be used? As a short skirt— still wrapped around the wearer and not stepped into—but separated from the plaid, it is first mentioned in 1698. It is generally agreed that it was tolerably common before the 1745 Rising but the evidence for its use much before that date is very scanty. In a description of Highland dress by Thomas Kirk, a Yorkshireman who made a tour of Scotland in 1677, it is not at all clear if the kilt was worn separately from the plaid. How did the separate kilt come into use? As it would obviously make for the easier movement of the wearer when at work, it could be supposed that at some time the invention of the kilt was due to a particular necessity. The claim that the small kilt was the invention of an Englishman was first set out in a letter written in 1768 and printed in 1785 in the *Edinburgh Magazine*. It appeared under the heading: 'The Felie-beg no part of the Ancient Highland Dress. Part of a letter from Ivan Baillie of Aberiachan, Esq'. In this it was stated that about fifty years previously Thomas Rawlinson, an Englishman, had been carrying out some iron work in Glengarry and Lochaber. He observed that his Highland workmen found the use of the full Highland dress very cumbersome, yet if they left off their plaids they appeared almost naked. Rawlinson therefore directed that the lower pleated part of what was called the kilt should be used while the upper part was laid aside, in other words the small kilt or feliebeg was made as seen today, eg, on soldiers in Highland regiments, without the upper part.

This account of the origin of the small kilt has caused Highlanders and other Scotsmen to become very indignant, as though it were an attack on Highland customs and traditions. If the antiquity of the small kilt could be established, the story would be demonstrably inaccurate, but it is pointed out by students of Highland costume that the first pictorial evidence of the existence of the little kilt is provided in a portrait of the Young Glengarry—Alasdair Ruadh MacDonell, who died in 1761. This portrait, which is in private possession but reproduced in J. Telfer Dunbar's *History of Highland Dress* (plate 22 and pp 69–70), shows Young Glengarry accompanied by a henchman who wears a scarlet short coat and waistcoat with a red tartan small kilt. This last garment was described as 'the first specimen of this reduced member of the belted plaid with which we are acquainted, and which like all others of the original form is plaited throughout its entire circumference'.

The suggestion that an Englishman invented the small kilt cannot be proved or disproved but Scottish writers point out several facts which have a bearing on the matter. The letter in which the claim was made has a respectable antiquity of 200 years, going back to the date (1782) when the Parliamentary ban on Highland dress was removed. Moreover, and of the utmost importance, the story was not put forward by an Englishman, but originated with a Scot and has been supported by Scots of great experience in Highland manners. As to the identity of the writer of the letter, Ivan Baillie, the following account is given by J. G. Mackay in his book *The Romantic Story of the Highland Garb and the Tartan* (1924), p 209. 'Evan Baillie of Aberiachan [a place on Loch Ness] was son of Alexander Baillie of Dochfer, and brother of William Baillie of Rosehall, County Sutherland, who gave much useful information during 1745–6, and uncle of Major Hugh Robert Duff, whose wife was the only daughter of Arthur Forbes of Culloden.'

In his letter, Baillie stated categorically that he had known Rawlinson in about 1728. Moreover, he added, 'and I certify from my own knowledge that till I returned from Edinburgh to reside in this country in the year 1725 . . . I never saw the *felie-beg* used, nor heard any mention of such a piece of dress, not [even] from my father, who was very intelligent and well-known to the Highlanders, and lived to the age of 83 years and died in the year 1738, born in May 1655'.

Baillie was a Writer to the Signet (the title of some Scottish solicitors) so should have been careful in assessing evidence. He added that he used 'f' and not 'ph' in spelling *felie-beg*, 'as in my esteem, more adapted to the Gaelic'.

Other writers give the same story independently. Thus, an

editor of Camden's *Britannia*, brought out in 1789, refers to the kilt, or *feliebeg*, as a 'little plaid or short petticoat reaching to the knees, substituted of late to the longer end of the plaid'.

Sir John Sinclair (born in 1754) who was a Highlander living on his Highland estates and president of the Highland Society in London, stated very clearly: 'It is well known that the phillibeg was invented by an Englishman in Lochaber about 60 years ago, he naturally thought his workmen could be more active in that light petticoat than in the belted plaid, and that it was more decent to wear it than to have no clothing at all, which was the case with some of those employed by him in cutting down the woods in Lochaber'. He assigned the date of the invention to about 1730.

John Maccullough is also mentioned as writing in 1824 that the kilt had been invented by an Englishman named Rawlinson, though he locates him in Perthshire as a lead miner.

It is unlikely that a local invention, whether in Lochaber or in Perthshire, would have spread so quickly all over the Highlands, and another fact of great importance is the first appearance, so far as is known, of the little kilt in connection with a Glengarry henchman. It was in Glengarry and Lochaber that Rawlinson was working some years before the painting of the Young Glengarry portrait. John Sobieski Stuart, who is dealt with in a later chapter, was the author of a massive work, *The Costume of the Clans*, published in 1845. This writer, who lived in the Highlands, repeated the story that the kilt was an English invention—though he said that two Englishmen were responsible. The statement could have been merely repetition, but something more valuable was added by Sobieski Stuart. 'The new garment immediately attracted the notice of Ian MacAlasdair Mhir Raonnill of Glengarry', who had succeeded to the chieftainship in 1720. The subject of our portrait is none other than his son, Alasdair Ruadh of Glengarry. Both the Sobieski Stuart brothers were friends and guests of the Glengarry of their day, who confirmed the story of his ancestor and the kilt. Does the picture of Alasdair Ruadh and his henchman in the kilt strengthen the tradition? It well might.'[4]

There the matter must rest. As to the supposed antiquity of the kilt the early seventeenth century may be taken as a period of transition from the old Irish dress to the belted plaid. We have, for instance, a print of a German broadsheet of 1631 showing four Highlanders who were probably men of Mackay's Regiment, serving under the Swedish king, Gustavus Adolphus. These four men are depicted as wearing clothes of tartan pattern. They have bonnets and plaids, but three of them have their legs covered by very long garments. No kilt is worn, not even as part of a belted plaid. The fourth man wears a long, voluminous garment, with his legs bare, while the others appear to have brogues. Incidentally, two of them carry bows and arrows, a third a musket. In the background are other Highlanders who appear to be wearing belted plaids or kilts to the knee. The description on the print is that the men are: *Irrländer oder Irren*, ie, Irishmen, probably because the clothes reminded the artist of having seen the Irish (Mackay's men were wearing a development of Irish dress), plus the fact that the Gaelic language was then being described by many writers as Irish. The further evolution of the belted plaid is demonstrated in the very interesting drawings of soldiers of the Black Watch, made in 1743, by the artist Van der Gucht.

The development from the Irish shirt or mantle to the belted plaid is perhaps best summed-up by Alexander Machain, who edited W. F. Skene's *The Highlanders of Scotland* (1902), and who said that the bare knee custom is really a southern European dress and not the 'garb of old Gaul', which he described as breeches. He added that the kilt (meaning, of course, the belted plaid, the big kilt) was invented in the Lowland wars of the seventeenth and eighteenth centuries. Possibly 'Continental' should be substituted for 'Lowland', since thousands of Scottish soldiers served foreign powers in that period. To which may be added the views of Sir John Sinclair, who has been mentioned above. In 1794, he raised the Rothesay and Caithness Fencibles and, convinced that trews or tartan trunk hose were much older than the kilt, he dressed his Fencibles accordingly.

> Let others boast of philibeg
> Of kilt and belted plaid
> Whilst we the ancient trews will wear,
> In which our fathers bled.[5]

Not historically accurate, but it does show that a distinguished Highlander, loyal to the traditions of his race, regarded the feliebeg as a comparatively late invention. It was worn well before the '45, but evidence of much earlier use cannot be established.

There remains the subject of tartan. The modern interpretation of it is: 'material woven in stripes or bands of various colours, combinations of which are repeated at regular intervals forming symmetrical patterns, the pattern of the warp and woof being the same' ('Early Tartans', J. Telfer Dunbar, *Old Highland Dress, etc*, p 63).

Parti- or various-coloured garments are mentioned by many writers in describing Highland clothes, and there is nothing surprising about the use of different colours in the same garments. The fashion is to be seen in many parts of the world, and it could be said that a rudimentary kind of tartan pattern existed in many places beside the Highlands.

Everyone is familiar with the styles of tartans of the various clans. Clan books with potted histories and brilliant illustrations are to be found in most libraries and bookshops. The clan tartans are sometimes, perhaps often, claimed as of great antiquity but the plain fact is that they are not. There is overwhelming pictorial evidence to show that while tartan patterns were certainly worn before the '45, when the identity of the wearer's clan is known the pattern of the tartan shown in a picture or other illustration does not conform to that now firmly associated with the clan or the chief of the line in question.

It was at one time usual to explain this startling discrepancy as being due to the thirty-five-year ban on Highland dress from 1747 to 1782 during which the older women of the clan died off, without being able to hand down to their daughters their knowledge of the weaving of the tartan and their skill in dyeing the cloth. Hence, it was said, the variations when the weaving of tartan was resumed.

This explanation does not agree with the facts. Many portraits of chiefs and clansmen were in existence before the '45. To take one example, that of Alastair Grant, the Champion, which was painted by Richard Waitt in 1714. In colour and pattern the tartan shown does not agree with any modern clan tartan. The Grants are an anciently-recorded clan claiming descent from the royal line of King Kenneth MacAlpin. In the

'45 the clan supported both Hanoverian and Stuart, most being loyal to George II, while Grant of Glenmoriston was out for Prince Charles. This being so, the bulk of the clan had continuity so that knowledge of the tartan should have been preserved. Now, no less than ten portraits exist of members of the Grant family (including in the total one of the chief's piper, William Cumming), all at Grant Castle in Morayshire. With one exception they are dated not later than 1725; most of them were made in 1713–14, and one (of Mungo Grant of Mallochhard) is undated. The verdict of an expert on the tartans painted in the pictures is: 'As to the tartans of the foregoing ten portraits, the first two of which are full-length portraits and the remainder to the waist only, suffice it to say that not only do all the tartans vary, but except for the first two, none of them resemble the present-day Grant tartans. The two portraits of the Laird's Piper and Champion slightly resemble a modern Grant pattern and this could well be taken as an attempt at uniform tartan in the following or "tail" of a chief.' (J. Telfer Dunbar, op cit, p 70.) It may be added that the Grant chiefs ordered all their armed followers to wear tartan coats of red and green, but no mention was made of a clan Grant tartan.

Varieties of tartan were often worn by the same person, as evidenced by a pre-1746 picture of the MacDonald children, which shows four different tartans, only the colours of which are similar; or, again, in a portrait of Lord Duffus in which the tartans are varied and differ from modern patterns. In the 1719 portrait of Donald Grant of Glenbeg, painted by Richard Waitt, the tartan is striped in one direction only. Altogether, the impression gained from the pre-1746 tartan illustrations is that the wearers chose their tartan in accordance with their own predilections and had no objection to wearing two or three different designs.

The most striking example of the latter phenomenon is seen in David Morier's famous battle picture of Culloden, in which the Highlanders are seen attacking Barrell's Regiment. This is no fanciful expression of an artist's view of how a close combat should have gone. The artist, a Swiss, was commissioned by the Duke of Cumberland to paint a battle scene at Culloden, and as he had previously made a very careful series of pictures of a soldier from each regiment of the British Army, his portrayal of Barrell's Regiment is likely to have been accurate. Particularly as he was allowed to use some of the prisoners as models. In this battle picture he painted it is clear that the eight Highlanders shown are wearing at least twenty-three different tartans, none of which can be identified with present-day patterns.

Two explanations are offered for this. One is that different clans were mixed up in the heat of action. But 23 divided by 8 would mean that some clansmen were wearing more than one tartan. The other explanation is that besides the chief's tartan, each man wore maternal and paternal tartans. This seems unlikely and, in any case, disproves the belief in an immutable clan tartan. The white cockade was the mark of the Jacobites and the clan badge in the bonnet that of the particular clan.

Clan tartans, then, were not settled before the '45; indeed, they are a product of the period following the repeal of the ban on Highland dress, and more particularly of that era in the nineteenth century which saw such a great revival of interest in things Highland. The idea of life in the Highlands having been unchanging, and of immemorial antiquity makes for some unforgettable passages in Lord Macaulay's *History of England* but is not, by any stretch of fact, entirely correct.

Change is indicated, too, in the matter of the Highlander's weapons. In olden days, before 1500, the Highland sword was a large two-handed weapon with a blade five feet long. The weapon used in the famous combat on the North Inch, it demanded the user's full strength and, of course, no shield could be used with it. It had a terrible killing power, but several disadvantages in close combat; a nimble antagonist who avoided the first blow could get within the guard of the wielder and strike at him before he could recover from the blow he had aimed. An instance of this is described by Sir Walter Scott in the encounter between the young Englishman and the Swiss in *Anne of Geierstein.*

In the sixteenth century the clansmen used a shorter sword with a basket-style hilt. This is the broadsword erroneously termed the claymore, which is, in fact, the name of the two-handed sword. A two-handed Scottish sword, 58½in long and known technically as the Lowland type, is preserved in the Tower of London Armouries and dates from the second half

E

of the sixteenth century. In the same collection there is a Scottish claymore of the early seventeenth century, 55$\frac{1}{10}$ in long and said to have been carried before the Old Pretender when he arrived in Scotland in 1715. Ceremonial use of such a large sword is feasible but it is most unlikely that so cumbersome a weapon was ever used in seventeenth-century warfare.

Other weapons of the Highlander were the dirk and Lochaber axe. The term 'dirk' begins to be used c 1600, and its meaning is not certain but it maintained its usefulness among the Highlanders up to the '45. The Lochaber axe was a weapon mounted on a haft or stave and was used in Scotland from the Middle Ages to the eighteenth century. It is described as having 'a cleaver-like blade with a convex cutting edge, often projecting beyond the top of the haft in an acute point. A curved fluke, or, more usually a hook, was normally attached to the back of the head; this could be used for scaling walls or for pulling down fascines'.[6]

The Highlanders of a later period (seventeenth to eighteenth centuries) carried a targe, or shield, made of wood and covered with bull's hide. Projecting from the middle of it was a steel spike. This defensive equipment could not be carried or used in conjunction with the two-handed sword, but proved of immense value to the clansmen in their battles with regular troops armed with musket and bayonet. The clansmen parried the bayonet on his targe, and cleft the opposing soldier with his broadsword on head or shoulder. At the same time the Highlander had his dirk ready in his left hand under his targe so that he could stab with it as well as cut with the broadsword.

As to weapons for use at a distance, the clans, like all their contemporaries, at first used bows and arrows. They were skilled in their use, and as hunting was a constant habit in the Highlands the clansmen had plenty of opportunities for practice. As firearms displaced archery the Highlanders acquired fowling pieces and muskets, the latter often of an old-fashioned type. They also used pistols.

In battle, the Highland tactics were simple but disconcerting to an opponent who was unused to them. Having advanced within range of the enemy, the Highlanders discharged their muskets, flung them down along with their plaids, gave a mighty shout and rushed forward. Their speed in approach was very fast and one can easily imagine how unnerving such an attack could be to troops who had never met anything like it before. The battles of the seventeenth and eighteenth centuries between Highlanders and government troops are of very great military interest and had a decisive effect on British army tactics.

No account of Highland ways could leave out the bagpipes whose music, to those who love the pipes, is the most inspiring of all. It is difficult to conceive of cowardice in warfare while the pipes are playing, and easy to understand such acts of heroism as at the storming of the Heights of Dargai, when the Gordons' regimental piper, shot in both legs, yet endured to play his pipes until his comrades gained the summit of the hill.

The bagpipes are found in many lands and are not original to the Scottish Highlands. Skene's editor (op cit, p 141) remarked of the instrument: 'It came to Scotland in the 14th century and reached the Highlands in the 16th century where it was hospitably received. Major (1521) does not mention it among Highland musical instruments, but Buchanan, 50 years later, says the Highlanders use it for war purposes. They also improved it by adding the big drone, whence the "Prob Mhor". It is thoroughly non-Gaelic in origin.'

Anciently, the harp was the great musical instrument of the Highlands, and was used by the bards who sang of the achievements of chiefs and of their clans. The King of Scots, as the Chief of Chiefs, had his Sennachie or clan historian whose duty it was to recount the King's ancestors at a coronation. It is from this office that that of the Lord Lyon of Scotland developed, the position being one of great antiquity.

It is a vexed question how far any of the old Gaelic poetry survived into modern times. It is certain that what did survive was very much under the influence of Irish literary culture and it is said that the literary language of the Highlands was Irish Gaelic. Under the repressive regime in Ireland in the seventeenth and eighteenth centuries, the Irish literary culture declined and passed away. The Highland literary culture likewise declined and, as with so many Highland matters, it was not until after the '45 and its ensuing troubles that Gaelic literature blossomed out.

An interesting literary controversy in 1760 centred around the alleged translation of the poems of Ossian, one of the old Celtic bards, by James Macpherson, a scholar and poet who lived 1736–96. He produced in 1760 a work under the heading *Fragments of Ancient Poetry collected in the Highlands of Scotland and translated from the Gaelic or Erse language.* At first the translations were welcomed with enthusiasm but their authenticity was soon impugned by Dr Samuel Johnson in England and by David Hume in Scotland. The obvious answer to the attacks was for Macpherson to produce his Gaelic originals, but this was never done and the manuscripts which he did leave behind have been destroyed. The general view now held is that if Macpherson did really find some old Gaelic MSS, they were not only scanty but completely overlaid by his own work. Even so, his work, slightly based on the original Gaelic though it may have been, had its part in the romantic movement in literature which arose in Britain and in Europe in the later eighteenth century. Bishop Percy's *Reliques of Ancient English Poetry* (1765) was another work which collected some of the older poetry. In this case the materials were genuine, but another precursor of the Romantic Revival, Thomas Chatterton, could not claim even the scanty original which lay behind Ossian. Chatterton, brought up in close association with the medieval splendours of St Mary Redcliffe's church in Bristol, used his undoubted poetic gifts under the guise of 'translations' from the alleged manuscripts of a monk named Rowley.

The remains of genuine Gaelic poetry and of other literature are indeed small, which is not so surprising when the turbulence of the area and the length of time are considered. One survival is the *Book of Deer*, so named from the monastery of that name in Aberdeenshire. Written between 1000 and 1100, this manuscript contains a Latin version of part of the Gospels, with notes in Latin and Gaelic mainly about such things as grants of land to the monastery. Other manuscripts in the Advocates' Library in Edinburgh, and dating between 1400 and 1600, are in Irish with the exception of *The Book of the Dean of Lismore*, though all were written in Scotland. The latter work is mostly in verse and consists of compositions of Irish and Scots bards. The contents were collected by Sir James MacGregor, Dean of Lismore in Argyllshire between 1512 and 1526. Irish metric forms are used in the poems and of these the Ossianic ballads in the Scotch Gaelic, amounting to some 2,500 lines, are the most important. Other survivals include the verses in *The Book of Fernaig*, compiled between 1688 and 1693 by Duncan Macrae and running to some 4,200 lines, and the *Red and Black Books of Clanranald*, written by the bards of the Clanranald chiefs and dealing with clan histories and the wars of Montrose.

There are ancient legends of Gaelic heroes, notably concerning Fingal and, as always with the old Highland life, linked with Ireland. One of the old myths connected the Giant's Causeway in Northern Ireland with Fingal's Cave in Staffa, in the Hebrides, the geological formation being the same in both places.

The ancient institution of tribal bards died out early in the eighteenth century, possibly because of the eclipse of the native Irish culture, and most of the literary monuments in the Gaelic language may be said to derive from the revival of Gaelic literature which followed the repression after the '45.

Building in the Highlands was generally very primitive, both in materials and style. The houses of the chiefs were naturally more spacious than those of their clansmen and some built castles of stone as residences as well as strongholds. But even as late as 1840, at the time of the Highland Clearances, it was only a matter almost of minutes to remove a family and their furniture and to burn the humble steading.

6 The Clans in the Sixteenth Century

THE PICTURE OF the Highlanders as a race apart from the rest of the Scots crystallised as early as the fourteenth century at least. John Fordun, who died in 1384, was part author of the *Scotichronicon* and continued it with his *Gesta Annalia*. He was probably a chantry priest of Aberdeen and collected materials for his writings in England and Ireland as well as Scotland from 1363 to 1384. A quotation from his Chronicles (vol 2, p 38) is given in volume 3 of Skene's *Celtic Scotland*:

> The manners and customs of the Scots vary with the diversity of their speech, for two languages are spoken amongst them, the Scottish and the Teutonic, the latter of which is the language of those who occupy the seaboard and plains, while the race of Scottish speech inhabits the highlands and outlying islands. The people of the coast are of domestic and civilized habits, trusty, patient and urbane, decent in their attire, affable and peaceful, devout in divine worship, yet always prone to resist a wrong at the hands of their enemies. The highlanders and people of the islands, on the other hand, are a savage and untamed nation, rude and independent, given to rapine, easeloving, of a docile and warm disposition, comely in person, but unsightly in dress, hostile to the English people and language, and owing to diversity of speech, even to their own nation, and exceedingly cruel. They are, however, faithful and obedient to their king and country and easily made to submit to law if properly governed.

With this may well be compared an opinion given nearly 600 years later. 'He found the Pathans "attractive with a sense of humour, and obviously men, though they often justified their reputation for cruelty and treachery"; men not dissimilar in many ways from the ancestors of his now comrades in the Black Watch—Highlanders as they were before the Industrial Revolution, the Clearances and other processes of civilisation had had their effect.' The above is from *Wavell, Scholar and Soldier* by

John Connell (1964, p 48), giving the first Earl Wavell's view of the Pathans.

Fordun's views represent a body of opinion which steadily hardened among Lowland Scots from the fourteenth century onwards, and it has been enshrined in a Gaelic proverb about the deadly hate of the Lowlander (that is the Sassenach) for the Gael. One of the most recently written books on Scotland's history also gives expression to this 600-year-old conception of the Highlanders. The author thinks that Perth might have been a better capital for Scotland than Edinburgh, as the latter was too remote from the northern and Celtic parts of the country and too close to English attack. 'If Perth had become Scotland's capital it could have lived and grown without the recurrent punishment that Edinburgh suffered, and a government lodged on the Highland Line might have acquired some sympathy with the *splendid savages* who shared its country, and realised the advantage of uniting them in interest with Lowlanders who were as turbulent as Clan Donald, but increasingly aware of a changing world and the profit to be wrung from peaceful commerce.' (Eric Linklater, *The Royal House of Scotland*, 1970, pp 20–21. The italics are mine, L.G.P.)

Not to labour the point of view of the Lowlanders, only one more reference need be given. In the terrible failure of the attempted colonisation of Darien in 1698–99, the settlers expressed themselves thus: 'Near on a third at least are wild Highlanders that cannot speak or understand Scotch, which are barbarians to us and we to them.' (John Prebble, *The Darien Disaster*, 1968, p 250.) It is no wonder that foreign writers, English or Continental, should express the same views. In most cases they visited Edinburgh or the Lowlands first and were there indoctrinated about the wildmen of the hills, though, in fact, the accounts given by English writers are not as damaging to the Highlanders' reputation as those of the Lowland Scots.

That Fordun's description of Highland ways is inconsistent is perfectly obvious. A people so inured as he and later Scots writers allege to murder, cruelty and rapine, are yet, according to Fordun, possessed of many virtues. Indeed, the clansmen are described as docile and amenable to law, *if properly governed.*

That proviso was the key and it was never applied. The story of the Scottish monarchy and of Scotland is one of the progressive decline of the Celtic element from the thirteenth century to the eighteenth. Alexander III was the last of the old race of kings descended in the male line from Kenneth Mac-Alpin. He was succeeded by Anglo-Norman barons, a description applicable to the Balliol and Bruce; descended it is true through the female side from the old Celtic monarchs but with sympathies and outlook largely directed to the feudalism of the south, which was completely at variance with the clan system.

When King Robert the Bruce's male line failed and the first of the Stuarts came to the throne, the breach between Highland and Lowland widened even more. To make matters worse, there was the constant threat in the fourteenth and fifteenth centuries to the sovereignty of the Scots kings by the Lords of the Isles, and even when the Lords of the Isles had been overthrown, the Highlands did not become quiet and peaceable. There was the feud between Clan Chattan and its enemy (possibly the Camerons) which culminated in the combat on the North Inch. Such blood feuds could persist over the generations.

The Stuart kings from James I (1406–37) to James VI (1567–1625) were, with the exception of James III, able rulers, but they were pursued by a fate more malignant than that which attended any other race of kings. They all succeeded to the throne as minors, and during their minorities regents misruled for their own ends. To kidnap the boy king and to hold him in a virtual captivity was the object of factions among the nobles. Then, on the young king reaching an age when he could assert himself, there was usually an Act of Parliament to resume any lands which had been alienated from the Crown; generally there were trials of various noble offenders, followed sometimes by executions, and almost always by forfeiture of estates. As the King did not possess a standing army, or the money with which English sovereigns hired mercenaries or paid their own subjects as regular soldiers, he had to rely on playing off one mighty subject against another. Nor did the Scots king have the administrative machinery which would have enabled him to control for the benefit of his realm the huge estates which came to him from the forfeitures of traitorous nobles. Consequently, the King had no alternative but, after a few years, to pass over the estates to another of the great lords in the hope that he would prove more loyal.

Even more disastrous was the liability to accident and sudden death of the Stuart line. James I was murdered after a reign of twelve years—he began to rule effectively in 1424. James II, who succeeded at the age of six, was killed by the explosion of a cannon when he was thirty. His son, James III, was murdered after the battle of Sauchieburn in 1488, and James IV was killed at Flodden in 1513. James V died in 1542 of a broken heart after the rout of Solway Moss. He had succeeded his father at the age of one and died when he was twenty-nine. His daughter Mary (Queen of Scots) succeeded when she was only a week old, and had her head cut off in 1587 after spending nineteen years in captivity in England. Her son, James VI, was by all showing the most successful of the whole dynasty. He managed to die in his bed, having been (nominally at first), a king from 1567 to 1625. James VI became James I of England and thus united the two crowns. He also succeeded, with the power which he acquired in England, in pacifying the Scottish border country.

Obviously, rulers who suffered from so many disabilities could not be expected to bring order to the Highlands. The Lowlands, too, were the scene of violent animosities, contempt of the law, bloodshed and rapine. Having no police force, and no army other than feudal contingents supplied by nobles who in a short while would themselves become law-breakers, the Scots kings did as well as could be expected.

The usual policy adopted by these kings towards their Highland subjects was that of force tempered by guile. James I had already dealt with the Duke of Albany and his relatives before turning his attention to the Highland chiefs. Albany was the King's cousin but that did not save him from being executed at the King's command along with several of his family. Some were tortured before being executed—five of the younger Albany's men were torn to pieces by wild horses. And when James called upon the chiefs to meet him at a parliament at Inverness in 1427 some forty of them were seized, imprisoned and hanged. A few of the chiefs did not fall into the trap, among them one of the MacDonald chieftains, John Mhor of Islay, ancestor of Earls of Antrim, who feared to come to Inverness. He did not escape death. The King sent James Campbell to fetch him and, possibly in pursuance of some personal grudge against Islay, Campbell found and slew him. Whether James's justice was even-handed we cannot tell, but Campbell was duly executed, though the King appears to have been quite pleased with the removal of Islay.

The idea behind these forceful proceedings was to intimidate the leaders, both Lowland and Highland. It did not succeed. Continual disturbances agitated the Highlands, clan battles were frequent and did not cease until the last male Stuart left the throne in 1688.

During the reign of James IV, when the independence of the Lords of the Isles was nearly at an end, the King determined to overawe the Highlanders with the splendour of his court and the might of his power. Among his many other accomplishments, he spoke Gaelic, along with Latin, Spanish, French, German, Flemish and Italian.[1] In 1490, accompanied by his court, he went across the mountains from Perth from the Mearns in Renfrewshire to Loch Rannoch. In 1493 he twice visited the Highlands, going as far as Dunstaffnage and Mengarry in Ardnamurchan. In 1494 he went three times to the western isles, travelling with a large fleet the splendour of whose equipment was matched only by the appearance of those sailing with the sovereign.

It may be thought that a policy of conciliatory measures and a bestowal of favours rather than one of force might better have succeeded in pacifying the Highlands, and to some extent James IV did try such a policy and became on good terms with many of the chiefs. But with his death there was reversion to the older methods of force, and of attempts to divide the chiefs and so keep them at loggerheads with each other. This may partly have been due to the belief that James's policy had not worked, and certainly there were still quarrels among the clans and frequent minor disturbances of the peace. Even during James IV's great progress in 1494, one of the MacDonalds, the chief of Islay, showed his contempt for the Crown. 'Dunaverty in South Kintyre, he [ie, King James IV] also seized to the prejudice of John of Islay. . . . Just as James was departing, John of Islay captured the castle, and hung the governor in full sight of the King.' (Lang, *History*, vol 1, p 366.) It was too gross an insult to be stomached, and soon afterwards James got MacIan of Ardnamurchan to capture Islay's sons and they were hanged on the Borough Moor of Edinburgh. It may be an understatement to say that the King's writ did not run smoothly in the western Highlands and the Isles.

The Highlanders were patriotic enough to follow James to the greatest defeat in Scottish annals, Flodden. Under their leaders, Argyll and Lennox, they made a furious charge against Sir Edward Stanley, only to be shattered. The Highland charge was to achieve spectacular successes in the seventeenth and eighteenth centuries against troops armed with musket and bayonet, but it was not by any means uniformly successful in earlier days when Lowlanders or English wore armour and carried powerful weapons. The English at Flodden were well-armed and among their weapons was the formidable English bill, which could be just as useful in holding off an enemy as in cutting him down. Nor could Scottish archery ever match that of the English. Still, although both Argyll and Lennox fell and the Highlanders fled, they had accompanied their king on his campaign into England, half a kingdom away from their homeland. In this connection it should be remembered that, in the next great clash with the English, the Highlanders are credited with supplying 10,000 men to the Scots army. This was at Pinkie in 1547. It has also to be recorded that in the defeat the Highlanders were the first to flee.

Two deductions are to be made from the presence and the behaviour of the clans at such important battles as Bannockburn, Flodden and Pinkie. They responded with outstanding loyalty to the call of the King of Scots and came readily to fight on behalf of their country, although they knew themselves to be hated and despised by the Lowlanders. The second consideration is their comparative failure in battle. Braver and hardier than their opponents though they were, and skilled as they were in the use of their weapons, they did not achieve many victories against southern enemies. Harlaw was not a Highland triumph and, as we have seen, the Lord of the Isles was forced to retreat.

During the rest of the sixteenth century, after Flodden, the history of the Highlands is a melancholy story of murderous incidents, and of the Government's reaction to them. Very often in Scotland a law-breaker would be put to the horn, that is proclaimed an outlaw, which meant that any man could kill him. The usual result was that the outlaw went on living as before, especially if he lived among a strong body of kinsfolk, and this was particularly so in the Highlands.

In desperation, the Scottish government would order the virtual or even declared extermination of a clan, but in the absence of police or army it was impossible to have such sentences carried out any more than outlawry could be enforced. The only way to give effect to the order was to commission the enemies of that particular clan to carry out the sentence, for the Highlanders, like the Indian tribes of North America, lived very much in a constant state of inter-clan warfare.

The Scottish government, ie, the monarchy, tried the method of employing great nobles as Lord Lieutenants, and in the sixty years between James V's death and James VI's accession to the English throne, two great nobles, the Earl of Argyll, head of the house of Campbell, and the Earl of Huntly, head of the Gordons, were employed in this way.[2] The trouble with this arrangement was that while it might in the short term stop some disorders, it also paved the way for future blood feuds. Thus, when the Campbells became the most important clan after the fall of the Lords of the Isles, they also secured a liberal share of Highland hatred, simply because they emerged from each civil war with control of more territory.

A brief chronicle of events in the reigns of James V, Mary and James VI will show the disordered state of the Highlands at that time. In 1516 there was a contest between John and Donald Mackay, the bastards of Y-Roy-Mackay, and the latter's brother, Neill, to secure possession of the Mackay lands in Strathnaver in Sutherland. The Earl of Caithness supported Neill and with this assistance he obtained control of the Mackay country. John Mackay in the meantime had secured the help of Clan Chattan, while Donald made headway against Neill. Donald ambushed Neill's forces and killed both his sons and most of their men. On John's return he and Donald had Neill beheaded by his own foster-brother. In 1517 the Mackay brothers invaded Sutherland but were repelled by the Earl's forces with great loss. Over 250 of the Mackay following were killed, and 38 of the Sutherland men, numbers which should be borne in mind for comparison with later conflicts such as the famous Massacre of Glencoe. According to Sir Robert Gordon, the battle in 1517 was the greatest yet fought in the Sutherland-Caithness area.[3]

Soon after this incident the Gunns took their revenge upon the Keiths for a treachery they had suffered very many years earlier. There had long been a feud between them which it was decided to settle by a meeting of twelve from each side. The rendezvous was the Chapel of St Tayr in Caithness, near Girnighoe. The twelve were to come to the meeting on horseback. The Gunns arrived first and went to pray in the chapel. When the Keiths arrived they had two men on each of the twelve horses, and in the ensuing fight all the Gunns were killed. This was in 1464 and in about 1520 the grandson of the Gunn chief killed George Keith of Aikregell, together with his son and twelve of his followers.

There were yet other disturbances between John Mackay and the Murrays, involving minor battles and loss of life, and then, in 1526, trouble arose in the Clan Chattan. The chief and head of the clan was Lauchlan MacKintosh of Dunnachtan, who was murdered by his kinsman, James Malcolmson. The clan pursued him with his followers to Rothiemurchus in Inverness-shire and killed them. The late chief's son being only a child, the clan elected the chief's bastard brother, Hector MacKintosh, to act as chief or as the title went, captain, until his nephew came of age. The Earl of Moray undertook the care and education of the boy but Hector wished to get him into his own power. In the course of attempting this, Hector and his followers committed many acts of violence, including the slaughter of twenty-four Ogilvies. The King, James V, then a boy of thirteen, acting on the advice of his council, granted the Earl of Moray powers to stop the law-breaking of the MacKintoshes. The Earl pursued and defeated MacKintosh and his men, 300 of whom he captured and hanged, but he could not find Hector MacKintosh and none of his clansmen would reveal his retreat. 'Their faith was so true to their captain, that they could not be persuaded either by fair means or by any terror of death, to break the same or to betray their master' (Sir R. Gordon). The sequel yet further illustrates the dis-

turbed condition of the Highlands. Hector MacKintosh submitted to the King and his submission was accepted. Soon
afterwards he was killed in St Andrews by a man called James
Spence, who was beheaded for his crime. Well educated under
the Earl of Moray, the young MacKintosh chief was a good
young man who had tried to administer his clan in peace. His
murderer was his nearest kinsman who, not liking his policy,
killed him.

One of the chiefs who had been imprisoned by James IV was
Ian Moydertach, the Captain of Clanranald. In 1531 and 1534
he received charters from the Crown in which he was recognised as chief of the clan. The reason for use of such documents,
'sheepskin grants' as they were contemptuously called by the
older chiefs, was to try to instil into the minds of the Highland
leaders the conception that they held their lands and position
as vassals of the Crown. In the case of this Clanranald chief, the
charters were a recognition of the unsurpation by Moydertach
of the chiefship. The last regular chief had been murdered by
his own people, his young sons set aside, and one of his uncles
appointed by the clan as chief. Moydertach was this uncle's
natural son. But charters or no charters, his succession was not
to pass without opposition, and a half-brother of Moydertach's
father, named Ranald Gallda, tried to obtain the headship of
the clan.

Ranald had been reared by his mother's family, the Frazers,
of whom Lord Lovat, the chief of the Frazers, had been appointed by James V as the royal lieutenant in place of the Earl
of Huntly. By Lovat's manoeuvres, the charters to Moydertach
were withdrawn and re-granted to Ranald Gallda, but it was
not long before he was driven out by Moydertach with the aid
of Keppoch and Lochiel, who then ravaged Lovat's lands. Once
again Lovat, with the help of Huntly, imposed Ranald Gallda
upon the clan. On the way back to their own country the Frazers,
who numbered some 300, saw the Clanranald descending from
a hill near Loch Lochy. It was 3 July and the weather being
hot, the Frazers stripped to their shirts, hence the name of the
battle, Blar-Nan-Leine, the battle of the shirts. The combat was
very fierce. Nearly all the Frazers were slain, including Lord
Lovat and his heir, the Master of Lovat, a youth just returned
from the University of Paris. Ranald Gallda had accompanied

his friends and was also killed. The story goes that the clan Frazer would have been wiped out, were it not that the wives of eighty of the clan were pregnant and each bore a male child.

That battle was in 1544, and in retaliation for the defeat of the Frazers, the Earl of Huntly invaded Clanranald territory, captured many of the leading men of the tribe and put them to death. Meanwhile, MacKintosh, acting on behalf of Huntly, had captured Keppoch and Lochiel, who had been allies of Moydertach. Both these chiefs were at feud with MacKintosh, so that he was able to gratify his revenge by handing them over to Huntly. They were both executed in 1546. Three years later MacKintosh was accused of conspiring against Huntly's life and was executed.

As for Moydertach, he was in the end able to keep his headship of the clan and his charters. He was proclaimed an outlaw but no one bothered to enforce the sentence, and he finally secured a pardon.

After the death of James V, the Queen, Mary of Guise, the 'French widow', became Regent and herself undertook a journey into the Highlands to try to put a stop to the disorders. The usual government expedient was followed, several chiefs were imprisoned and other law-breakers brought to trial, condemned and executed.

During these times the Earls of Argyll were advancing their fortunes. The 6th Earl, unlike most of his house, believed in harsh and forceful measures. He imprisoned without legal warrant John Maclean, son of a former chief of that clan and, as head of the house of Campbell, invaded the lands of Maclean of Duart. The latter was in the Lowlands receiving his education, one of the early examples of chiefs being educated away from the Highlands. The young chief suspected his Tutor of paying more attention to his own interests, and of having spread it abroad that Duart would become soft from a Sassenach education. On returning home, Duart put the Tutor, who was also his kinsman and foster-father, in irons for a long while, until he finally had his head cut off. A young chief of such a manly and realistic approach soon rid his lands of the Campbells, and then made an alliance with them to attack the Macdonalds of Glengarry.

So the wearisome catalogue of crime continued, and in the

twelve years before his accession to England's throne James VI had his time very much occupied with two sources of trouble in the Lowlands, his turbulent nobles and the new religion of Presbyterianism. On the whole he did well in dealing with both difficulties, but it must have been with a sigh of relief that he hastened to cross the Border on his way to London.

James VI and I was, unlike the other Stuarts, a timorous man. He did not care to look upon a sword, even when knighting one of his own subjects, but did not object to stern physical measures being taken by others. He did not lead military expeditions to the Highlands, but entrusted his lieutenants with far-reaching powers. Among the various Acts passed in his reign for the good ordering of the disturbed areas was an Act of 1597 which required the production of proofs of holdings, rather like the English Statute of Frauds in 1677. In Scotland, an Act of this type could only lead to fresh oppression, as it could be used by great men to goad the chiefs and clans into rebellion, the suppression of which legalised forfeiture of their lands.

Another Act, in 1581, actually gave legal sanction to the blood feud by allowing action to be taken against a fellow clansman when the offender himself could not be found. Along with other measures, the Act also authorised the taking of hostages for security of good behaviour.

The dissension between Protestants and Catholics was yet another cause of trouble. After the establishment of the Presbyterian form of church government, many Highlanders were in rebellion under the Earl of Huntly, who was a Catholic. The Earl of Argyll was given a commission to subdue him but failed signally when he was soundly beaten at the fiercely contested battle of Glenlivet.

It was then decided that James VI himself should go into the Highlands, and some of the Gordon strongholds were taken. Argyll retrieved his fortunes by subduing the rebels, but as the King thought him likely to go too far in crushing Huntly, he recalled him, and Argyll was accordingly warded—to use the expressive Scots phrase—in Edinburgh Castle.

Some of the characters mentioned above pursued their eventful and bloody careers to what must appear almost predestined ends. MacIan of Ardnamurchan was engaged to Lochiel's daughter, but was murdered by a kinsman. Maclean of Duart was Lochiel's uncle, and though he gave shelter to the murderer he could not save him from being killed by some of the Camerons. Hence a feud between Maclean and Cameron. The life of Duart ended in a battle with the Macdonalds, and in his dying declaration he besought his uncle, Lochiel, to avenge him. In return for so acting Lochiel was made subject to forfeiture, and Hay, Mackenzie, Glengarry, Maclean and Argyll all put in claims to the Lochiel inheritance. Lochiel was feign to surrender to his neighbours the outlying portions of his estates while securing their help to retain the rest.

The inter-tribal battles do not make for interesting narrative and the best commentary on them comes from a contemporary of many of the struggles. Writing of troubles in the north, Sir Robert Gordon said:

> The long, the many, the horrible encounters which happened between these two tribes, with the bloodshed and infinite spoils committed in every part of Caithness by them and their associates, are of disordered and troublesome memory, that, what with their asperous names, together with the confusion of place, times, and persons, would yet be a war to the reader to overlook them; and therefore to favour mine own pains and his who should get little profit or delight thereby, I do pass them over.

Wearisome and monotonous in their narrative the feuds and battles of the clans undoubtedly were, and so, too, were the letters of fire and sword issued by the King's Council against different tribes. Like the sentences of outlawry, such measures of extermination could only be carried out by the use of force on the part of the delinquents' neighbours and, in the case of clans, 'it proved impossible to crush one rebellious house without the risk of raising up another upon the ruins' (*The Loyal Clans*, Audrey Cunningham, 1932, p 34). This was true in the Lowlands and, if anything, more so in the Highlands.

Moreover, when the Government ordered the rooting-out of a clan, it usually only intended some harsh measure to be taken against it, and before extremities were reached the letters of condemnation would be withdrawn, along with the commission which had been issued to the executioners.

There was, however, one clan whose extermination really was attempted. It failed, but not for want of trying on the part of the Government or of those to whom the task was entrusted. This clan was that of Macgregor, which still flourishes and

F

whose present head is a British baronet. Though the plan failed, the history of this attempt to destroy the Macgregors is of great interest as showing the state of life in the Highlands at the end of the sixteenth century and the opening of the seventeenth, just before the departure of James VI to take possession of his new English kingdom.

The clan Gregor has for its motto 'Royal is my race' and its tradition relates that it descends from Griogar, the third son of King Alpin. When the clan chiefs appear in history, they are seen as rulers of Glenorchy in north-east Inverness-shire. In their earlier and more prosperous period the Macgregors possessed large territories in Argyllshire and Perthshire, in Glenstrae and Glenlochy, Glenyon and Glengyle. These wide areas were owned on the old clan principle, probably from a very remote period, but needless to say without charters. The Macgregors had the misfortune to suffer under the introduction of feudal and legalistic principles by their neighbours, the Campbells, and so became involved in the familiar pattern in which clansmen owed rents to a landlord who was not their chief, while their deep-seated loyalty lay with their clan superior. Conflicts arising from this situation were inevitable, but the Macgregors were unique owing to three factors: not only the Campbells, but several other landlords impinged upon Macgregor territory; the Macgregor country was ideally situated geographically for raids on lowland areas and for speedy retreat into difficult fastnesses; and, last of all, the Macgregors had a fighting spirit which refused to submit to unjust treatment. As more and more of their lands were taken and their clansmen became broken men, without a croft to till, cattle to mind, or a miserable shelter for wife and bairns, the Macgregors tended to become ready helpers in any raid or outrage which was going.

The Macgregor country lay athwart the Highlands from Callander in Perthshire over and above the lands from Stirling to the Clyde. The country in front of them offered a tempting prey, while behind them were the fastnesses of the central Highlands, providing 'a swift and sure retreat. The wilds of Loch Katrine or the vast moor of Rannock in the north were a refuge for the broken Macgregors, who had access by the great valleys of Glenorchy, Glendochart, Glenlyon and Glenogle to the rich cattle-breeding lands of the Menzies about Loch Tay, and on towards Perth, Doune, Stirling, Dumbarton and Glasgow' (Audrey Cunningham, op cit, p 134). As the work of government was conducted from Perth and Stirling as well as from Edinburgh, the Macgregors constituted a threat to the Government, as well as to the centre of Scotland.

The Macgregors soon acquired such a reputation for lawlessness that they were held to be principals in many depredations in which they were either not concerned or were not the chief actors. This attribution of misdeeds to the Macgregors is found as far back as 1544, when a collection of persons described in Scots as 'thieves, limmers, and sorners upon the lieges', and including a Campbell of Strachur, was considered to be mostly Macgregor in composition.

In the early part of the century the Campbells had succeeded in imposing Ian Macgregor of Glenstrae, chief of the clan Gregor Ciar, as head of the whole Macgregor clan, probably because he had married a daughter of Sir Colin Campbell of Glenorchy. The rightful line did not regain the headship of the clan until after 1774. The MacGregor intruded by Campbell of Glenorchy was the 7th chief. The 6th chief of the right line was buried on 26 May 1519, a day in which a great meteor was seen in Glenorchy. 'From that day', records the Chronicle, 'came the sad divisions and sorrows of the Gregarach.' Campbell friendship did not prove profitable to the clan. The clan chief, MacGregor of Glenstrae, was in the unenviable position of possessing lands whose area was quite insufficient to support those of his clansmen who came to him as broken men from other lost Macgregor properties. With the passage of the generations the chief of the Macgregors became a mere tenant of Campbell of Glenorchy. This was to prove fatal to the 10th chief, Gregor MacGregor of Glenstrae, grandson of the 7th chief. He was engaged in warfare against Campbell of Glenorchy, who had bought the superiority of Glenstrae. There were the customary raids and remission of penalties from the Crown; but James VI was only three years old at the time, and the Council acting in his name was not likely to take the part of a Highland chief against the great house of Campbell.

Campbell of Glenorchy eventually managed to capture MacGregor of Glenstrae and, with all the show of law on his side, arranged for the chief to be beheaded on 7 April 1570, at Balloch. Campbell invited Murray of Atholl and other distinguished guests to witness the execution.

An Act of 1587, known as the General Band, made landlords more responsible for the behaviour of their tenants and was the instrument by which the next Macgregor chief, the son of the executed man, was put out of his estates on the grounds that he was holding them against the proprietor's wishes. The Act of 1581 which had authorised reprisals against innocent clansmen for misdeeds of their guilty fellow clansmen, was invoked against the Macgregors who, in their desperation took full advantage of the barbarity of the measure, including killing thirteen Campbells to avenge their chief's execution.

So the clan's reckless behaviour continued and was steadily mounting to a climax when, in 1589, occurred a killing which brought the Macgregors into direct collision with the Crown. One branch of the clan led such wild and lonely lives in the cloud-capped mountains that they were known as the Children of Mist. Some of these wandering Macgregors killed John Drummond, one of the King's foresters; the exact reason is not known, but it would not be unlikely for a keeper of the King's deer to fall out with wandering outlaws. Still, it was a cardinal error to kill a servant of the Crown, engaged in protecting the King's sport, and far worse for the Children of the Mist to have brought his head to their chief, Macgregor of Glenstrae. To aggravate the offence, Drummond had been engaged in obtaining venison for the festivities to mark the arrival of the future queen, Anne of Denmark. Macgregor called together the whole clan in the church of Balquhidder, where each man laid his hand upon the dead forester's head, swearing to share the blood guilt and not to reveal the killer's identity.

The MacGregor chief was duly denounced along with 128 of his clansmen by the Council, and commission was issued to the various justices in the Macgregor country to proceed against them. There were many mutual animosities among the commissioners, the measures taken against the clan were quite ineffective and some two years later, in 1591–2, the MacGregor chief was granted a pardon. He then took legal action against some of the persecutors and even won a law action, being awarded damages against the Maclean of Duart. In 1596 Mac-

Gregor gave a bond for his good behaviour before King and Council.

The final cause of the outlawry of the Macgregors stemmed from a quarrel between them and the Colquhouns of Luss, Dumbartonshire. One of the MacGregor of Glenstrae's kinsfolk, Duncan, made a heavy raid on Luss territory in which he carried away 300 cows, 100 horses, 400 sheep, 400 goats, together with household effects. Two of the Colquhouns were slain, and in an attempt to play upon King James's sympathy, the Colquhoun women displayed before him the bloody shirts of their killed and wounded menfolk. According to the Macgregors, the number of shirts was multiplied by exhibiting some that had been dyed in sheep's blood. This was in 1602 and James lost no time in granting a commission to the Laird of Luss to proceed against the Macgregors on his own account and without reference to the Earl of Argyll, who had made a failure of the previous commission.

There are conflicting accounts of the events which followed in the early months of 1603. According to one story, Glenstrae had decided to try and settle matters peaceably with Luss. To this end, accompanied by some 200 clansmen, he had gone into the Lennox, Luss country, to make up the quarrel with the Colquhoun leader. The latter was suspicious of Glenstrae's intentions and summoned his own followers to the number of 300 horse and 500 foot, so that he would have sufficient force to cut off the Macgregors if the proposed peace conference should fail. In another version, two Macgregor pedlars are said to have trespassed on Luss property and to have been hanged in consequence, whereupon their chief at the head of 300 men demanded compensation. This being refused, a battle took place. Yet another version refers to a conference being held and of failure to reach agreement, whereupon the Macgregors began to march homeward but were followed by Luss with the intention of bringing them to battle.

Whatever the explanation, there is no doubt about the battle of Glenfruin, one of the bloodiest in clan history, which occurred in the early part of 1603. Glenstrae divided his forces into two, putting the smaller party under the command of his brother John. This section of the Macgregor force worked its way to the rear of the Colquhouns, and when the battle was at its height and the Colquhouns fully engaged with Glenstrae's men, the party led by John fell upon their rear. The Colquhouns were taken completely by surprise and driven from the battlefield with heavy loss. Over 200 were killed from Luss's side; of the Macgregors only two were killed, one being John, the chief's brother, who died from an arrow wound.

Some tales passed down by tradition about Glenfruin are too good to pass over. Glenstrae had, it is said, a foster-brother, a huge man covered with grey hair and called 'The Giant Mouse Man'. A body of students from Glasgow University had come to see the Macgregors routed (another version makes them citizens from Dumbarton, and some burgesses from that town were present and were killed), and these spectators are supposed to have been captured by Glenstrae and put in charge of his foster-brother. The latter's hairy body excited the ribald humour of the students, until the giant could endure no more. He despatched and buried them in a rude kind of tumulus, to which he pointed when asked by Glenstrae where they were.

If shirts had moved King James on the earlier occasion, he must have been completely horrified when the eleven score bloody shirts of the Colquhoun victims were exhibited before him. There, too, traditions differ, and some accounts claim that it was on this occasion, and not that of the earlier raid, that the march of the bereaved took place, with each widow or orphan wearing the shirt of the deceased husband or father. If so, there would have been no need of sheep's blood then.

James had learned in March that his cousin, Elizabeth I, had died, leaving him her throne and he was excitedly preparing for his departure to England. Before doing so, he found time to have an Act passed by the Scots Privy Council by which the whole clan Gregor was outlawed and the name of Macgregor proscribed for all time on pain of death. Not only were the fighters at Glenfruin to be outlawed, but even Macgregors who had taken no part in the battle and who were living peaceably had to change their surname. The penalty for disobedience was death and the killing of any Macgregor who persisted in using the name would be considered as legally permissible. No member of the clan was to carry weapons, and only a pointless knife was to be allowed for use at meals. Not more than four of the clan were permitted to meet together. No agreement or contract made with a Macgregor was to be considered legal, and no child of the name could be christened. Penalties as savage as these, branding the innocent along with the guilty, had never been pronounced in earlier instances, and it was only the existence of so many avowed enemies of the Macgregors that made their imposition possible in this case.

Details of the resultant hunting-down of the Macgregors are revolting even by the standards of Highland or Scottish brutalities. 'There were sums of £1,000 Scots each, paid to Lochiel, Clanranald and Lawers for various purposes, rewards for heads, and a sum of £100 to Archibald Armstrong for attending His Majesty's service with "larg doggis" against the clan Gregor.' (Audrey Cunningham, op cit, p 160.)[4] In hunting down the clansmen, some were bribed to betray the others, and one man, Robert Abroch, originally a Macgregor, made the long journey to London to see King James VI and offer to serve against his own people. Abroch was a man who had committed robberies with murder, one of his victims having been no less a person than Campbell of Glenorchy. The King's reply to his offer was that he could be received to mercy at the price of not less than half a dozen heads of slaughtered Macgregors.

In the event, Abroch was cautioned and allowed to return to Scotland, where he changed his name to Ramsay and put himself under the protection of Sir Lauchlin Mackintosh, who is said to have used him to attack an enemy of his own. Later he left the Clan Chattan territory and, in about 1621, was leader of a band in the Lennox which terrorised the country. Finally, finding things becoming too hot for him, he made a dramatic surrender to the Lord Chancellor at Perth, and got away with his life on condition that he agreed to serve in the King's army overseas. Others of the clan went with him and vanished from history. In this they were but following the example of many thousands of Scots, not only Highlanders, who served in Europe's wars in the seventeenth century. Many did not return to Scotland but founded families with a tradition of Scottish origins, in Sweden, Austria, Germany, Poland and other countries.

In the efforts made to exterminate the Macgregors, the 11th chief, Alastair MacGregor of Glenstrae, was sought out with special ferocity. He had been captured by Campbell of Ard-

kinglas but escaped from him soon after the battle of Glenfruin.
Realising that he had small chance of remaining permanently
at liberty, he surrendered to the Earl of Argyll on the strict
condition that he should be conducted to England, where he
hoped to appear before the King and put his case in full. To
ensure this, he gave thirty of the best men in his clan to be
held hostage as guarantors of his return to Scotland. His
captors kept to the letter of their word by taking him to Berwick which then, as now, counted as part of England. Then he
was brought back to Edinburgh, tried and, a foregone conclusion, condemned to death. According to some historians all
the thirty hostages were executed with their chief; other writers
are more moderate and content themselves with stating that,
along with the chief, four clansmen who had stood trial with
him were hanged, together with seven hostages who had stood
no trial and were reputed to be honest men. The gallows was
built in the form of a cross and the chief had the highest place.

As for the women and children of the clan, the women were
to be branded or transported; boys over fourteen were to be
taken to Ireland (now one of King James's new kingdoms) and
let out as herdsmen, death to be their penalty if they returned
to Scotland. Other barbaric penalties were ordained for boys
who did not go to Ireland, or who escaped from custody. These
measures, or at least not all of them, may not have been carried
out owing to the scruples of conscience, or caution, of those to
whom the women and children were committed.

Ten years after Glenfruin, Argyll thought that he had cleared
up the majority of the Macgregors. He was mistaken. The clan
refused to die, and was soon to give ample proof of its fighting
power. During the time of the 12th chief (nephew of the unfortunate 11th), the clan, along with its chief, were simply
broken wanderers in the hills, but the 13th chief, brother of the
12th, was more fortunate. He declared for Montrose when he
raised the royal standard in 1644 and was promised that in
return for their services the clan's disabilities would be removed.
Loyally then did the Macgregors fight for the Stuarts who had
condemned them to extinction. At the Restoration of Charles II
they were rewarded by the removal of their disabilities. An
Act of Repeal passed in 1661 stated that 'considering that those
who were formerly designed by the name of Macgregor had

during the troubles carried themselves with such loyalty and affection to his Majesty as might justly wipe off all memory of their former miscarriages, and take off all mark of reproach put upon them for the same'.[5]

So, for the next thirty-two years the Macgregors could once again proudly use their own surname. The Act did not, however, restore their lands and they were obliged to subsist in very difficult circumstances, while their chief lived on an island in Loch Rannoch which he held by the sword. With no ancestral lands on which to live, the Macgregors were almost bound to be involved in cattle raiding and other depredations, and in 1671 they joined with the Macdonalds of Glencoe and Keppoch in raiding the Menzies lands. No doubt enemies of the Macregors were quick to point to this exploit as yet another example of the clansmen's inveterate bad habits, and the result was the issue to Menzies and Campbell of Glenarchy of one of the customary 'fire and sword' commissions against the clan.

The Macgregors remained loyal to the Stuarts in exile, and suffered for it through the re-enactment of the penal laws against them in 1693. These were not repealed until 1774-5, so that taking the two periods of proscription together, the Macgregors were under the ban for 139 years, and lived as a broken clan for 170 years, the best part of two centuries.

Yet their numerous enemies did not, in the end, prevail against them. In 1775 no less than 826 clansmen came forward to declare themselves as Macgregors and to acknowledge John Murray of Lanrick as their chief. He became Sir John Murray MacGregor of MacGregor, 1st Baronet, and 18th Chief. He, of course, resumed the surname of his race, as did his clansmen. That so many persons should, after close on 200 years of persecution, still proudly call themselves Macgregors is proof enough of the soundness of their stock and ancestry. Indeed, it has been said that 'they are perhaps the only clan who can be reasonably certain that all who bear the surname are genuine scions of the ancient chiefly blood, while some branches [such as are probably the Marquesses of Londonderry] have never yet resumed their proud patronymic.' (*Burke's Peerage*, MacGregor, Bart.)

What of the famous Rob Roy, or 'Red Robert' MacGregor, who has been portrayed in Scott's romance very much as a

Highland Robin Hood? His pedigree is somewhat involved. Sir Walter Scott describes him as being descended from the Giant Mouse Man, previously mentioned. 'Rob Roy Mac-Gregor Campbell', he wrote, 'which last name he bore in consequence of the Acts of Parliament abolishing his own, was the younger son of Donald MacGregor of Glengyle, said to have been a lieutenant colonel [probably in the service of James II], by his wife, a daughter of Campbell of Glenfalloch.' To this Scott adds that Rob Roy acquired some sort of property on the east side of Loch Lomond. He is described by Sir Thomas Innes of Learney as 'a son of MacGregor of Glengyle by a sister of the notorious Capt Robert Campbell of Glenlyon'. Deprived of his lands by quarrels with the House of Montrose, Rob Roy became a prominent Jacobite and his exploits form a vivid chapter in Highland romance.

Rob Roy was originally a drover, conducting a legitimate trade. He had borrowed some money from the Duke of Montrose and, being unable to pay, ran away. In 1712 he was prosecuted because of his debts, and in the course of trying to get the money the Duke's agents abused his wife. Whereupon Rob collected a band of followers and henceforth lived by raiding the Duke's cattle, which he sold in another part of the country. He was a sort of client of the Duke of Argyll who gave him a measure of protection. Despite all the efforts of his enemies, Rob succeeded in dying in his bed. When his end was near and he heard that an enemy was coming to see him, he insisted on being propped up in bed, with his broadsword, dirk and pistols at hand. The interview was conducted with cold courtesy and when the unwelcome visitor had gone, Rob relaxed, saying, 'Now all is over, let the piper play the dirge', and died before it was completed.

Such is the unhappy history of the illustrious Macgregor clan, illuminated, however, by a constant display of tenacious courage and refusal to admit defeat. Other families, like Ruthven, had their names abolished and many were ordered to be wiped out, but 'the exceptional persistence and thoroughness with which the persecution of the Macgregors was maintained was due to other causes than the ferocity of the Council.' (Cunningham, op cit, p 166.)

In the present chapter the history of the Macgregors has been carried to its conclusion, exceeding the limits of the sixteenth century. In the next, it will be seen that with the union of the Crowns, and above all the exile of the Stuart kings, the fortunes of the clans declined to their ultimate ruin.

7 The Clans in the Seventeenth Century to 1685

THE UNION OF the Crowns made James VI ruler of three kingdoms instead of Scotland alone. Difficulties in England, of a financial and political nature, which had been growing under Elizabeth I became much more serious when a new dynasty was on the English throne. The last of the Stuart family to reign, Queen Anne, died in 1714, and the greater part of the seventeenth century was taken up with the struggle between Parliament and the forces which it represented versus the Crown. Along with social and economic changes which made direct personal rule by the monarch much more difficult than under the Tudors, there went a great religious revolution. Despite occasional conflicts between Church and State, the organisation of the Catholic Church had generally upheld the monarchical principle. In England, this was true of the established Anglican Church after the Reformation, but the movement initiated by the Protestant reformers brought about a much more independent approach to God. The personal relationship between God and each man's soul was far more pronounced under Protestantism than it had been under the Roman faith. Those who had learnt to criticise the ancient Church were soon to criticise other institutions.

In Scotland, the Presbyterian form of Protestantism gained control. James VI preferred the rule of his bishops and to some extent he restored episcopacy. Charles I was less fortunate and the upshot of the religious convulsions of the century in Scotland was the establishment of the Presbyterian Kirk as the official church of the country. In England, the independent religious movement which objected to the retention of episcopacy in the State church was not able to gain control, except under the Commonwealth (1649–60). The Puritans did, however, have a permanent influence on English life. After 1660 a section of the population of England, destined to grow to half, was outside the national church. In politics, the Puritan revolution eventually brought about constitutional monarchy in place of personal rule by the sovereign, and succeeded in substituting first a Dutch prince and then the House of Hanover in place of the male Stuarts.

Throughout the whole period, not only of the seventeenth century but for the 150 years from 1603 to 1747, the Highland clans supplied the only effective force on which the Stuarts could rely. In the civil war between Charles I and the Parliament in 1644–5, it was the Highlanders who formed Montrose's army and enabled him to win a series of brilliant victories. In 1689 it was Highlanders who won at Killiecrankie. In 1715 they constituted the (for Highlanders) large army of 12,000 under the Earl of Mar. They also rose again in the abortive attempt at invasion by only 300 Spanish troops in 1719. Finally it was overwhelmingly the Highlanders who fought the '45 for Prince Charles.

What motive induced the clans to imperil their lives, families and homes for the Stuarts? The issuing of letters of fire and sword, the penalties of outlawry and forfeiture, were all in the King's name. James I, James IV, James V and James VI had been united on one feature of their policy—harsh, often underhanded treatment of the chiefs. Yet the ancient patriarchal system of clan life made the clansmen regard the King as their Chief of Chiefs, a paternal figure. Occasionally there were bad chiefs; they were sometimes deposed, sometimes helped out of chiefship and life by ambitious kinsmen, but the institution of chiefship survived and the clansmen gave implicit obedience to their chief. A similar loyalty was felt to the King, who was more often thought of as King of Scots, ie, of the people, rather than as King of Scotland, the feudal lord and owner of the whole realm.

Many instances occurred in which chiefs whose conduct had been really outrageous, could yet come in, make their submission and be received back into favour. The harsh measures decreed by Crown and Council were carried out, in so far as they were efficient, by great men like the Earl of Argyll or the Earl of Huntly, who had personal and pecuniary interests in spoliation of a clan. Hence direct rule by the King was felt to be much better than that of his lieutenants and not so inimical to the clan system.

Nor was it. James VI's theory of the divine right of kings was a paternalist theory and with it went the idea of the King as a Christian leader responsible to God for the spiritual welfare of his people. Equally, paternal chiefs were easier to fit into this theory than reactionary feudal lords or moneyed magnates. In the last years of his rule in Scotland and during the first years he reigned in England, James VI was feeling his way towards treating his Highland subjects much better than ever before. In the course of this new treatment the King experienced a very unpleasant setback, but one from which he learnt some salutary lessons.

One of James's ideas was for the plantation or colonisation of an area which had long been regarded as wild or infertile but whose poorness, he felt, was largely the fault of the inhabitants. On a large scale, when the plantation of Ulster in Northern Ireland was attempted in 1611, James's conception was realised. The natives were subdued or driven out and the settlers who were brought in proved their ability to colonise.

Earlier than this, however, in 1598, an attempt to colonise the island of Lewis was a failure. The King, and many others with him, were under the delusion that the Highlands and Islands could be made highly productive. The native population, they thought, were idle and shiftless and needed the presence of more energetic and industrious people who would show them how to cultivate the soil and develop the natural resources. The problem of Highland development remains after four and a half centuries. The Highlanders were not idle in the Lowland sense; they did not spend their days drinking usquebaugh, and awaking from stupor only to prosecute a blood feud. In fact, they produced and cultivated the best their glens could supply.

In the Lewis experiment, the Adventurers of Fife obtained full powers from James to take over the island, expropriate the clan Macleod who were the owners, and make it a fruitful colony. In this expedition, men and women from the east of the kingdom set out for an island on the west of Scotland very much in the spirit and with the outlook of those who, not more than a generation afterwards, were to voyage to New England. There was the same expectation of hardships to be endured, of encounters with fierce and hostile savages speaking a barbaric tongue, and the same expectation of ultimate prosperity.

The venture was a complete failure, despite the provision of everything needful for the colony, and financial aid from several wealthy men whom the King had persuaded to support the project. A large number of artisans and a body of soldiers went to Lewis where they erected a small town, again as did the settlers in New England, but their arrival united the Macleods, who had been quarrelling for some sixty years over the question of chiefship, and they proceeded to make things very difficult for the adventurers. The project languished until 1605 when efforts were renewed, but among other mistakes the colonists made was that of double-dealing against the Macleod leaders. The latter then fell back upon their old and tried methods and drove the colonists out of the island by force.

James's next attempt to colonise the islands was better conceived, and was prefaced by the visit in 1609 of a commission headed by the Bishop of the Isles. By then, James was armed with the power which possession of England gave him and could supply English naval forces and Irish soldiers to aid his men in the Isles. He had already succeeded in bringing more peace to the Border country than it had ever known, and was genuinely concerned for the good of his subjects. Above all, there had been a great change of attitude towards the Highlanders. The idea of extirpating them tribe by tribe had been discarded. Industry and religion were to be taught to the clansmen, and education was to be encouraged. In place of the Irish tongue, English was to be taught and the native language abolished. There was to be no more resorting to the old feudal methods whereby one law-breaker was employed to deprive those who were slightly worse than himself of life and land.

There was, however, one relapse into the older methods for which the commissioners associated with the Bishop of the Isles could scarcely be blamed. This breach in the new policy was caused by the Macdonalds who were in feud with the Macleans. MacDonald of Islay got Maclean of Duart into his power with about eighty of the latter's clansmen. Islay proceeded to kill them at the rate of two per day because he thought that the Macleans had murdered his brother at Duart. The Maclean chief was saved by the Council but the early success of the Bishop's mission was seriously jeopardised by Macdonald's recourse to arms.

In the opening of the 1609 commission everything went well. Lord Ochiltree, who represented the secular arm, had a large military and naval force at his command and the chiefs came to Islay and Mull to make their submission. They were taken on board the main vessel of the fleet and told that they were to hear a sermon from the Bishop. Among the chiefs present were Maclean of Duart, Donald Gorm of Sleat, Clanranald, Macleod and Maclean of Ardgour; others promised their due appearance. Those on board the ship did listen to a sermon but soon realised that they were being taken away to periods of imprisonment at Edinburgh, Stirling or Dumbarton. Still, there were no executions, and the enlightened policy of the Government gave due consideration to the poorest of the clansmen, realising that these humble men had no mind other than that of the chiefs and gentlemen of the clan.

Soon afterwards there was a meeting in Iona of nine chiefs with the King's officers at which the chiefs signed the Band and Statutes of Icolmkill. Under this it was agreed that the chiefs should render obedience to the King in Church and State; practices contrary to the law were to be given up; known criminals in the clan were to be handed over to the proper authorities, and handfasting—a kind of companionate marriage for a year and a day—was to be renounced. Religion was to be supported, churches built, ministers' stipends paid; idle persons were to be put to work. The children of the gentry were to be educated so that they could speak, read and write English. No attempt was made to undermine the authority of the chiefs, and there was no desire to do so. The King would rule the tribal areas directly, but the authority of the chiefs in matters not concerned with the common law of the realm would continue. The policy was good and may well have contributed much to the long-standing loyalty of many of the clans to the Stuart kings.

There is always a fascination in pondering over the hypo-

thetical in history. Had there been no civil war in Charles I's
reign, no Commonwealth, no fall of the Stuarts and no foreign
kings, what would have happened to the clans? It is possible
that, gradually, the clans could have been incorporated into
the body of the British people. Certainly, the measures set out
by James VI did have the effect of reducing some of their more
lawless habits. The leaders, the chiefs, became educated, and
in many cases cultured men, instead of savage chiefs knowing
only the blood feud and the clan battle. The last inter-tribal
conflict was at Mulroy in 1688, and was fought between the
Mackintoshes and Macdonalds.[1] It could well have been that
the clan system would have changed very slowly until it was
ultimately abolished as a mere relic of the past.

These are only speculations. The Stuart kings, unable to ad-
just themselves to the changing conditions in their English
kingdom, went into exile, and the most important sequel to
their attempts to regain the throne was the complete ruin of the
clan system. Instead of a slow decline which might have pro-
longed its relics into the nineteenth century, the system was
destined to a not-inglorious destruction on Drumossie Moor
(Culloden). Never again were the clansmen in arms. Hunted
down, robbed, massacred, outraged, the clans ceased to exist in
the old patriarchal sense. Defeated on the battlefield, savagely
attacked afterwards, their very dress prohibited and the rule
of their chiefs made illegal, the clans were finished. It is the
story of their gradually approaching doom that is the theme of
this and the next chapter.

In the convulsions resulting from the triumph of Presbyterianism in Scotland, the clans took no part. Some of them
adhered to the Catholic Church, some nominally embraced the
Kirk, but there was none of that interference by ministers in
political matters which was so characteristic of the Lowlands.
Had Charles I and his Church adviser, Archbishop Laud, been
more tactful and adroit they might have imposed an episcopal
system upon the Scots, with a fair conformity to the doctrine
and practice of the Church of England. Had Charles been a
better judge of men and been able to avoid embroilment with
his English Parliament, the Scottish religious settlement might
not have been so starkly Calvinistic. However, the fierce
Covenanting spirit of the Lowlands was completely wanting in

G

the Highlands. The only impact which it had was the strong reinforcement it gave to the deadly Sassenach hatred of the Gael. After centuries of separation by differences of language, manners and costume, Gael and Saxon were now yet further divided by religion. Even when the Highlanders were Presbyterians they did not, in the Lowlanders' view, show the same influences of the Spirit. The Lowlanders' conception of the Highland Scot was that of an uncouth barbarian unentitled to any fair or reasonable treatment. Faith was seldom kept with the clansmen and prisoners were slaughtered in cold blood. Even though Calvin's catechism had been translated into Gaelic in the days of James VI's conciliatory policy, the savage treatment of these so-called barbarians was still justified in the name of the Lord.[2] The behaviour of the Scottish Covenanters towards the clans can be compared with that of the English Puritans in North America. Imbued like their Scottish compeers with a rigid Calvinism, the English settlers of the future U.S.A. regarded the native Indians as vermin to be driven out or destroyed. Preaching the Gospel to them was unknown for a century and a half after the landing of the Pilgrim Fathers, though in French Canada the Catholic missionaries had laboured with the utmost self-sacrifice in the conversion of the Indians.

Although it was not until 1644 that the Highlanders impinged upon the Civil War, this is not to say that their lives passed without incident. Between 1613 and 1644 there were a number of disturbances in the Highlands, enough to keep them in a state of upheaval. In 1613 a serious rebellion broke out in the southern Hebrides—or so it was viewed by those in authority. It was part of the effort being made by the Macdonalds to retain part of the clan lands in Islay. The rising was suppressed by the 8th Earl (later Marquess) of Argyll. This was during the period when James VI was trying through the medium of the Bishop of the Isles to rule directly over the clans through their chiefs, and the use of Argyll was a reversion to the employment of great feudal officers more concerned with their own interests than with what sufferings they caused. Such was the attitude of Argyll and other great men of the Campbell family. In the course of his suppression of the clans, such as the clan Donald, Argyll incurred heavy expenses and was always in debt, sometimes to the extent of £30,000, then a huge sum. He appealed to Parliament, and both Scottish and English Parliaments made him grants of money, which were not always paid. There were even collections in church to assist him in defraying his debts! Yet debt-burdened as he was, Argyll was always able to find money to acquire titles to forfeited land in the clans' territories.

Other violent incidents occurred between the Earls of Caithness and of Sutherland respectively. In 1615, the Earl of Caithness suborned the heads of the clan Gunn to set fire to the cornfields of one, William Innes, with whom the Earl was at feud. His choice of the Gunns is the more interesting because he had caused the father of John Gunn, chief of the clan, to be hanged in 1586. With John Gunn and his brother, Alexander, came a cousin, Alexander Gunn. He was approached by the Earl first of all, but declined the task of firing the corn, considering it an ungentlemanly action. He was, however, prepared, he told the Earl, to murder William Innes, this being more honourable than fire-raising. The Earl then turned to the two brothers who agreed to set fire to the corn, whereupon the Earl gave out that it had been done by the Mackays. The affair was very long-drawn-out, and although two of the Gunns were examined by the Council, no effective action was taken. The incident is of interest as an example of the feuds between the clans and the lawlessness of the northern and western Highlands even when James VI could command an adequate force to carry out his wishes.

In 1624 there was another inter-clan conflict when the clan Chattan, in effect the Mackintoshes, fell out with the Earl of Moray. The clansmen took advantage of their chief being only a child to ravage the lands of Moray and his vassals but this particular trouble was settled without too much bloodshed. Soon afterwards, in 1628, feuds which had been simmering for a long time between the Grants came to open trouble. Nearly eighty years previously, John Grant of Ballindalloch had been murdered by John Roy Grant, a bastard son of John Grant of Glenmoriston, at the instigation of the chief of the clan, who hated Ballindalloch. In the course of this internecine struggle, many Grants of different branches of the clan were killed.

It was from these unruly elements, intensely suspicious and

jealous of one another, that James Graham, the 1st Marquess of Montrose, made an army which in one year—*annus mirabilis* indeed—conquered Scotland for Charles I. The Grahams are in origin a Lowland family whose records begin with a charter from King David I in the twelfth century. Although their name appears in clan books, they are not Highlanders, and certainly the first Marquess was not. It is of interest here to note that the three most successful leaders of the Highlanders were not clan chiefs but strangers: Montrose himself, his kinsman, Dundee (Claverhouse) and Bonnie Prince Charlie. All the three possessed attractive personalities and personal magnetism; there were chiefs of clans who were just as gifted but unable to command the allegiance of other clans.

In 1644, on 2 July, the King's army led by Prince Rupert had met with its first great defeat at Marston Moor. From this it never recovered. In the midst of his declining fortunes, Charles had turned to Montrose who in the previous year had offered to raise an army in Scotland for the royal cause. Charles at first declined but at the end of 1643 he agreed that Montrose should raise a force which was to be assisted by an Irish levy under the Earl of Antrim and a body of English cavalry. After the decline in the royal fortunes in England, the cavalry was not forthcoming and Montrose made his way through England and into Atholl. The bulk of the Scots army was then in England helping the Parliamentarians. It was commanded by General Leslie and consisted of soldiers as experienced as he was in the wars of the Continent. In Scotland, the Government commissioned Argyll, whom Charles had advanced to a marquessate in 1641, to raise an army, and he assembled a force of about 5,000 foot and 800 horse. With this army Argyll took Aberdeen and so frightened the then royal commander, the Marquess of Huntly, that he disbanded his forces and retired into private life. Everything looked hopeless for the King's cause with the passes into the Highlands, the key towns and forts all in the hands of the Covenanters. The only royalist who did not despair was Montrose. With two men, and himself disguised as a groom, he made his way to Tullibelton, in the hills near the Tay, and to a house belonging to a kinsman of his, Patrick Graham of Inchbrakie.[3]

While Montrose was meditating on the best way in which he

could effect his design, he received news that a force of 1,000
to 1,500 men had landed in the western Highlands. They were
led by Alexander Macdonald, the son of Coll MacGillespie of
Iona, a determined enemy of the house of Argyll. Macdonald
sent round the fiery cross but at first was joined only by the men
of his own clan. He did not know Montrose's whereabouts but
was able to communicate with him by letter. Montrose promised
Macdonald a general and ordered him to march into Atholl, in
Perthshire. When Montrose eventually met Macdonald he had
the satisfaction of receiving reinforcements from the Stewarts
and Robertsons, so that he had presently an army of 2,000 men.
Opposed to the royal cause were the Frasers, Grants, Rosses
and Monroes, under the leadership of the Earls of Sutherland
and Seaforth. These clans had threatened Macdonald's advance and their hostility is yet another instance of the disunity
of the clans.

Meanwhile Argyll, having burnt Macdonald's ships, was
following him up, but with much shorter marches, a feature of
Highland–Lowland warfare which was to be repeated in the
'45. No Highland force of any size had been seen in the Lowlands except as a contingent on the march with the rest of the
Scots army, but times had now changed, and the changes were
in favour of the Highland weapons. There were no long spears
as at Bannockburn, and no shields for the Lowland troops whose
muskets were awkward to handle and slow in use. Against these
was the terrible force of the Highland charge, the cleaving
power of the broadsword, and the use of the targe for parrying.

Montrose succeeded in winning over a small force sent against
him under the command of Lord Kilpont, heir to the Earl of
Menteith. The main Covenanting army was now at Perth and
Montrose decided to attack them before they could join up
with Argyll's force. The Covenanters had double Montrose's
3,000; he had neither artillery nor cavalry, he was short of
ammunition and, until they could obtain weapons from fallen
enemies, some of his Highlanders could do no better than use
stones off the moor which, in the event, did great execution
against the Covenanters' cavalry. The Highland tactics were
the same as they were to be 100 years later at Prestonpans; a
discharge of weapons at fairly close range, a fearsome shout
followed by a charge of amazing swiftness and an assault with

broadsword and Lochaber axe. The Covenanters gave way completely, even the cavalry fled and Montrose had won his first battle. Perth was taken the same day and warlike stores in plenty were obtained.

Montrose knew that the army which had been destroyed outside Perth consisted of inexperienced raw troops, and that the approaching force of Argyll was of a superior stamp. He therefore turned to march across the Tay towards Dundee to gain more adherents from the northern clans. On the way occurred an incident always liable to happen in clan armies. James Stewart of Ardvoirlick proposed to Lord Kilpont that they should murder Montrose. On Kilpont disagreeing, Stewart killed him and fled to Argyll. Montrose's army was reduced by the departure of Kilpont's followers with his body, and also by the dispersal to their homes of some of the clansmen with their booty. Still, with some 1,600 men, Montrose went on to encounter the Covenanting force at Aberdeen. A battle took place in which the Covenanters had the advantage of cavalry and cannon, but again they were utterly worsted by the fierceness with which the Highlanders and Irish rushed upon them. There was a great slaughter and Montrose's men entered Aberdeen on the heels of the fugitives, with the result that many of the citizens were slain and the town sacked. Montrose did not restrain his men, because a drummer he had sent to the burgesses under a flag of truce had been wantonly killed by them. The Covenanters complained bitterly of the conduct of Montrose's cruel Irish as they called them, who would strip a man of his clothes before killing him. In the sequel, Lowland treatment of the Irish was to be no less cruel.

Montrose was not able, despite his great successes, to attract the Gordons to his standard, because their chief, the Marquess of Huntly, was jealous of Montrose, who had superseded him as royal commander-in-chief in Scotland.

Argyll now brought his army up to Aberdeen and marched in search of Montrose, who was manoeuvring in the mountains. Some weeks followed of desultory skirmishing and of attempts by Argyll to parley with Montrose. The parleys were meant only to detach from Montrose's standard those who could be tempted by his offers, and Argyll was only too successful in enticing Montrose's Lowland officers. Montrose, however, had now decided upon a winter campaign in Argyll's home country, a feat which Argyll himself and most other people thought impossible, a Campbell saying, 'It's a far cry to Loch Awe', being a reference to the proverbial strength which its seclusion afforded the Argyll home. By maintaining a force of clansmen several thousand strong, Argyll was able to intimidate the nearby clans and prevent them from joining the King's standard.

Montrose divided his forces into two bodies. With the Irish and the men of Atholl, he went to Loch Tay and thence through Breadalbane. The clan Donald and other Highlanders went by a different route with instructions to meet him on the borders of Argyll. The Campbell country was defended by passes, the entry to which Argyll imagined to be unknown to his enemies. He left them unguarded, although on the news of Montrose's approach he had hurried from Edinburgh to his castle at Inverary. He thought Montrose to be about 100 miles distant when he was startled by the arrival of some shepherds who reported the enemy to be within two miles of Argyll's home. At once the Marquess consulted his own safety by boarding a fishing-boat on Loch Fyne and returning to the Lowlands. The Campbells were unable to offer any concerted opposition to the three parties into which Montrose divided his army and for about six weeks, from mid-December 1644 to the end of January 1645, his men did immense damage in the Campbell territory, ravaging it systematically.

At the end of this unprecedented devastation of Argyllshire, Montrose marched north-eastward toward Loch Ness with a view to capturing Inverness. On the way he was joined by the Farquharsons, some of the Gordons and others. An army of some 5,000 marched to meet him under the Earl of Seaforth, and Montrose was preparing for the encounter when, near the present Fort Augustus, he learned that Argyll with 3,000 men was laying Lochaber waste. Instead of marching back to meet Argyll, Montrose executed, in the dead of winter, a march across the snow-clad mountains between Glenroy and Ben Nevis, and was in Glennevis before Argyll knew of his arrival.

Argyll was a great hand at statecraft and business, but not a good soldier. He was often accused of cowardice and now, once again, he looked to his own security and took refuge on a boat in the nearby loch. When his army realised that there was a force on the heights above them, they thought it was composed of local inhabitants and not of Montrose's men—until the blare of his trumpets and the advance of his array showed that the seemingly impossible had been accomplished. Montrose had crossed the allegedly impassible mountains, a feat that only an irregular force could have achieved. The left wing of Montrose's Highlanders launched a furious assault on Argyll's centre and right wing, while Montrose's left wing similarly attacked Argyll's right which gave way and fled. The whole of the centre and left wing of the Campbell army made a feeble, ill-directed discharge of muskets and then ran away. More than 1,500 men, including several Campbell gentlemen of note, were killed and many of the fugitives were drowned in Loch Eil.

After the great victory of Inverlochy, Montrose returned to the north, across the mountains of Lochaber into Badenoch. Finding Inverness garrisoned, he marched towards Elgin, where he was joined by the Laird of Grant and some of the Moray men. The inhabitants of Elgin paid 4,000 marks in order to save their town, but when Montrose's men entered it they destroyed all the furniture in the houses out of irritation at finding that everything else had been removed. Some of the Gordon chiefs now joined Montrose, bringing him an accession of about 700 men. Entering Banff, Montrose allowed his army to plunder the place and it is recorded that they left nothing in the town which could be removed and took the clothes off every man they met in the streets. When he reached Turriff, Montrose received a deputation from the city of Aberdeen begging him not to let the Irish troops into the walls. This he agreed to but, in return, forced many of the Aberdonians to take weapons and join him.

Next, Montrose fenced with an army commanded by an experienced soldier, General Baillie, and after a series of marches and counter-marches, he decided to take Dundee, which had refused to open to him after his victory at Tippermuir. Dundee was stormed and sacked: 'The sack of the town continued till the evening, and the inhabitants were subjected to every excess which an infuriated and victorious soldiery, maddened by intoxication, could inflict.' (J. S. Keltie, *History of the Scottish Highlands*, vol 1, p 206.)

The devastation of Dundee was nearly the ruin of Montrose. He was an extremely able commander, not at all the brilliant exponent of headlong charges, but the main body of his army consisted of adventurers and it is remarkable that he was able to restrain them at all. Baillie advanced towards Dundee with 4,000 men and reached the gates just as Montrose had succeeded in disengaging the last of his men from the other side of the city. It was only by stupendous exertions that Montrose and his men were able to elude the pursuing Baillie, by-passing his army in the night, marching without sleep for two nights and covering a distance of forty miles in seventeen hours to gain the shelter of the Grampians.

Soon after this at Auldearn, about three miles to the southeast of Nairn, Montrose completely defeated the army of General Hurry, which contained a strong detachment of veteran troops. Baillie then advanced, joined up with Hurry and the remains of his army, and set off after Montrose. Again Montrose eluded him. His ability to move faster than his enemies was due to the mobility of the Highlanders; the skill to bemuse his opponents and vanish from their neighbourhood was Montrose's own talent.

At last, on 2 July 1645, Montrose's and Bailie's armies met at Alford, on Deeside. A hotly-contested battle ended in the complete rout of the Covenanters, and Argyll escaped only with great difficulty. One of the best of Montrose's supporters, the young Lord Gordon, was killed in the battle.

After Alford, many of the Highlanders went home with their spoil, always one of Montrose's difficulties and one which, more than anything else, handicapped his operations. None the less, he gathered his remaining forces together and soon moved down from the Dee, being joined by some valuable accessions as he marched through Angus and Blairgowrie. These included his kinsman, Patrick Graham with the Atholl Highlanders, the Macleans, Clanranald, Macgregors and Macnabs, Stewarts of Appin, and other smaller clans.

The Scottish Parliament had withdrawn from Edinburgh because of the plague, and gone to Perth. Only the army of Baillie and Hurry stood between Montrose and complete victory. Montrose's numbers were good, 5,000 foot and 500 horse, and at Kilsyth they cut the Covenanting army to pieces with a huge slaughter. Edinburgh surrendered and Montrose was in control of Scotland.

Success did not last. Montrose received instructions from King Charles to march to the Borders, where he was to meet some of the Lowland royalists and a body of horse from England. Unfortunately, Montrose's Highlanders, the main strength of his army, demanded leave to return home to look after their families. Montrose could not refuse and about 3,000 of his best troops then left him. They had promised to return within forty days, but before that time was over Montrose's fortune had been reversed. On 4 September 1645 he began to move south with the remnants of his forces. He reached the Border country and was soon close to Leslie, the Covenanting general who had returned from England with a huge force. Montrose was sadly disappointed by the response of the Lowland and Border loyalists, who did little more than pay lip service to the royal cause, and some of whom, like the Earl of Roxburgh, were in fact traitors.

At length Montrose took up his quarters on the north bank of the Ettrick, at a place called Philiphaugh, where he was surprised by Leslie, and his army routed. He himself escaped into the Highlands, where he endeavoured to raise another force. Meanwhile, the Covenanters took savage vengeance on any of his people on whom they could lay hands. Among these were the women and children of the Irish soldiers, who were thrown over a bridge. Any who reached the banks were knocked back into the water until they drowned. According to one account any woman with child was ripped open. Two prisoners taken at Philliphaugh were hanged without trial and later, in Edinburgh, other royalists were executed, as the Scots ruling body, the Estates, felt that it no longer need fear Montrose.

In the meantime, Montrose had collected some 1,500 men in the Highlands and might have gained more but for the arrival of the most precise instructions from the King that he was to disband his army. He had no alternative but to obey, though he knew that the King was in the power of his enemies and not a free agent. Montrose had a price on his head but he evaded foes and false friends alike and got away to Norway. His Highlanders had returned to their homes, and such of the

Irish contingent who had not been killed at Philiphaugh went over to Ireland. General Leslie marched into the Highlands, and when he secured the surrender of a stronghold those who yielded were usually shot. The Marquess of Huntly was captured and imprisoned, and later executed after the execution of King Charles.

The subsequent fate of the Marquess is soon told. In an attempt to raise an army on behalf of the new king, Charles II, he arrived with a small force in the Orkneys at the beginning of March 1650. He crossed over to the mainland with about 1,500 men but was routed at Carbisdall and forced to save himself by flight. He was captured, taken to Edinburgh, tried and sentenced to be hanged. His body was cut up and the parts delivered to the chief cities of Scotland. The trunk was buried under the gallows, but after the Restoration it was interred in St Giles Cathedral where there is now the Graham monument.

The punishments which the triumphant Lowlanders would have inflicted on Montrose's Highlanders can be imagined, but deliverance for the Highlands was to come from a strange quarter. Although they had always refused to carry out his orders, the Scots were genuinely shocked to hear of Charles I's execution. He was their divinely-appointed king, descended from their ancient royal line, and in their eyes the English had committed sacrilege in killing him. Without much delay the Scots offered the Crown to Charles II, under very humiliating conditions. Still, they were prepared to fight for him and began to levy an army. The English thought it wise to take counter-measures and sent Cromwell with part of the New Model Army to invade Scotland. This was in July 1650. He made little progress until on 3 September a blunder by Leslie reversed the situation. The Scots army was destroyed and Cromwell was master of southern Scotland. The Scots did not give in but the General Assembly sat in Stirling Castle. Charles II tried to escape to the Highlands where, despite all their suffering, a body of loyal Highlanders were ready to rally round him. Charles, however, decided to trust to the Lowlanders, but still a large number of Highlanders came to join the Scottish army which was forming north of the Firth of Forth. Cromwell sent part of his army under General Lambert across the Forth to get behind the Scottish army, and in an engagement at Inverkeithing the Scots were defeated. In this battle the Macleans fought very bravely, losing their chief, Sir Hector Maclean of Duart, but not until his foster-brothers had all died beside him, each crying 'Another for Hector!'

Again the clans had rallied to the royal cause despite their general dislike for the Covenanters, and they formed a considerable part of the 14,000-strong army which marched to invade England. On 31 July 1651, the Scots evaded Cromwell and by a bold strike marched to the south. Here was proof that the clans, when raised to a pitch of fervour, would be ready to march far from their homeland. It was Charles's own scheme and he had told his council that, once in England, a host of loyalists would join him. In this he was to be grievously disappointed, but his southern march reached Worcester on the 22 August 1651. Cromwell had been seriously misled. He left General Monk with 5,000 men to reduce the rest of Scotland, while he himself, with 10,000 troops, marched towards York. Charles had taken the western road through Carlisle and Cromwell, though he had been outmanoeuvred, was quick to retrieve the situation. Concentrating his troops in the direction of Worcester, he arrived there on 28 August and assumed the command of some 30,000 men. The 3 September 1651, anniversary of Dunbar, was hailed by Cromwell as his crowning mercy. The royal army was destroyed and Charles II became a fugitive with a price on his head. At Worcester, the clans fought bravely, the Frasers and the Macleods particularly distinguishing themselves. The Macleods of Duart were almost annihilated and never again took up arms for the Stuarts. A few of the Highlanders got back to Scotland, but those who were not killed were shipped off as labourers to the English colonies in America.

Monk's army in Scotland is of the greatest importance in the story of the clans. In the long centuries-old struggle between England and Scotland, England had tried several times to subjugate Scotland, and under Cromwell's vigorous rule and his splendid New Model Army she succeeded. The British Isles were united as never before. From the Pentland Firth to the Tweed, the Scots were under alien rule, and it was a good rule. English judges came to administer the law. They were incorruptible and cut through the jargon of Scots law to give just and commonsense decisions. A free-trade area was established with no duties on goods crossing the Border. One nation was to be created. The Scots were to be absorbed into the English. An army of 20,000 men was quartered in Scotland, with garrisons in forts at various places.[4] Above all, the ministers of the Kirk were restrained from preaching about politics. The Crown lands were taken over for the Commonwealth and the same measures put in force as in England for the sequestration and forfeiture of estates of the cavaliers.

In the Highlands, the army of Monk found their most difficult task. Some bodies of Highlanders remained under arms and Monk sent three detachments of soldiers against them, one to cross the mountains from Inverness towards Lochaber, the second from Perth in the same direction, and a third force by sea from Kintyre. The Frasers came in, but in general the clans did not submit and the trouble they caused, added to the natural difficulties of the country, compelled the English troops to retire. Monk and his men were, however, persevering and in a later action against the Earl of Glencairn, who had raised an insurrection, the clans were defeated. The chiefs then submitted with the exception of Cameron of Lochiel, who maintained an inveterate hostility towards the English garrison which Monk had planted at Inverlochy (Fort William). On one occasion he ambushed a party of soldiers who were cutting wood and drove them to their ships, having, it is said, killed 138 of them for the loss of five Camerons. At another time he is supposed to have killed 100 of the garrison, only the officers having resisted— which does not sound much like the grim Puritan soldiers of the New Model. A ferocious incident, when Lochiel bit out the throat of an English officer, occurred during the attack on the woodcutters, and the bite, said Lochiel, was the sweetest he had ever taken.

In the end, Monk's moderation rather than force of arms prevailed. The Marquess of Argyll became surety for Lochiel and he was required only to give his word of honour to live in peace; an indemnity was offered for all past offences and compensation was paid for the damage done to Lochiel's tenants by the garrison.

Lochiel, in fact, got off on very easy terms. He and his clan were to lay down the arms they had borne for Charles II and to take them up again for the Commonwealth. This was done in a ceremony at Inverlochy and not only Lochiel's men, but other clans as well, were allowed by Monk to carry arms within their own borders for self-defence. No similar privilege was granted to the Lowlanders, who were deprived of their weapons.

Monk governed the Highlands through the chiefs and from 1653 to 1660 there was peace in the Highlands. It was admitted by the Scots themselves that the English Government was just, fair and orderly. One of the Scots wrote in all seriousness:

> It is not to be forgotten that from the year 1652 to the year 1660, there was great good done by the preaching of the Gospel in the west of Scotland, more than was observed to have been for twenty or thirty years before; a great many brought in to Christ Jesus by a saving work of conversion, which was occasioned through ministers preaching nothing at all that time but the Gospel and had left off to preach up parliaments, armies, leagues, resolutions and remonstrances which was much in use from the year 1638 till that time 1652. [Law's *Memorials*, quoted in Keltie, op cit, vol 1, p 291.]

Had the Covenanters been in control of Scotland during this period, they would, judging from their treatment of Montrose's followers, have reverted to the old policy of letters of fire and sword against the clans.

An English soldier writing home from the Highlands describes the houses as built of earth and turf, set low in the ground, mere coverings from the elements; the people generally, both men and women, wore plaids about their middles. In the things of God they were simple and ignorant and some of them as brutish as heathens, but many willing to learn.

However good the English government of Scotland, it was still that of aliens and the Scots were glad to see Monk lead his men back to England. The Restoration of Charles II was received with exuberant enthusiasm in Scotland, and the Highlanders as a whole were able to live peaceably under their restored king. But the King himself was careful never again to go to Scotland. From the time of his visit as a young man until the visit in 1822 of George IV, no British sovereign as sovereign, visited Scotland.

On Charles II's restoration, the Marquess of Argyll had hurried to London to congratulate the King, but he was too powerful a man for his previous opposition to the monarchy to be overlooked. He was not allowed an interview but was lodged in the Tower and later taken back to Scotland, tried, found guilty of treason and executed. He had his head struck off by the Maiden, a form of the guillotine, and it was impaled on the same spike which had borne the head of Montrose. He died on 27 May 1661, and some twenty-four years later, on 30 June 1685, his son was executed at the same place and in the same manner.

The house of Campbell was passing through a time of depression and unlikely to have the same influence. Yet in 1674 the Highlands were disturbed by quarrels between Argyll and the Macleans of Duart.

The death of the Marquess of Argyll for treason meant the attaining of his peerages, but in 1663, by the influence of the Duke of Lauderdale, his eldest son was restored in blood as Earl of Argyll, Lord Campbell, Lorne and Kintyre, but not to the marquessate. His father had bought up some debts of the laird of Maclean and when the earl failed to obtain repayment he sought to invoke armed force, but the Macleans proved too strong for him. The clans—Lamont, Macnaughton, Macdougall and Maclean—had been loyal to the Crown, and having been punished for it by the earl's father they had no love for the younger Argyll.

The main troubles of the restored monarchy were not with the Highlanders but with the stiffest sects of the Covenanters. Episcopal government in the church was again being imposed upon the Scots, and some of the Kirk leaders were as ready to endure martyrdom as they and their followers were to resist government by force of arms. The strength of the resistance was in the south-western shires, where one of the strictest sects had been founded by Richard Cameron who, although he bore a Highland name, was not a Highlander but the son of a Falkland tradesman. Andrew Lang remarks humorously that Cameron's lack of second sight confirmed his want of Highland blood.[5]

In order to control these Lowland fanatics who were as ready to die as to kill, the Scottish Government determined upon a singular remedy. The clansmen were untouched by the theological ferment of the south and equally unconcerned with the controversies of the day. When it was troubled by disturbances in the western counties, and lacking any standing force like Monk's army, the Government called on the clansmen to keep order. For this purpose some 8,000 clansmen were assembled at the end of 1677, led by Atholl and Perth, and with Linlithgow as principal commander.

This was the famous Highland Host which in January 1678 occupied Glasgow and much of the south. The Duke of Lauderdale,[6] who enjoyed the support of Charles II, was the chief man in Scotland at this time, but his expedient of bringing in the clans was not successful from the Government's point of view as the Lowland proprietors refused to agree to evict their Covenanting tenants. No rising took place while the clans were in the south, but if one had occurred, Lauderdale would have used the Host to repress it. The clansmen were at free quarters, they did not have to pay for their lodging and were allowed to plunder. Nor were there any disturbances while they were encamped in Clydesdale, Renfrewshire, Kyle, Carrick and other Lowland districts. The inhabitants were afraid of the strangers, whose appearance and speech were so peculiar to them, and though the Covenanting Lowlanders complained of terrible actions by the clansmen, it is generally agreed that none of the Covenanters or dissenters lost their lives.

From the Highlanders' point of view the expedition was well worth while and by the time they were ordered home at the end of February 1678, they had gathered an enormous booty. Over a thousand dwellings had been looted and all sorts of household goods taken, horses being commandeered to carry the heavier items. On passing Stirling bridge each man drew his sword to show the world that they had returned unconquered from their enemies' land. They also had the unusual satisfaction of knowing that they had not been on a raid but acting as agents of the Government.

After the withdrawal of the Host, a rebellion did break out the following year, 1678, and the rebels were successful at Drumclog, against John Graham of Claverhouse and his cavalry, but not long afterwards the Duke of Monmouth, in command of a larger force, completely defeated the rebels and it was the severe punishments which followed that earned Claverhouse his nickname of 'Bloody Clavers'. Later, as Viscount Dundee, he was to gain a brilliant victory at the head of the clans.

This suppression of the Whig revolt by Monmouth and Claverhouse was followed in 1682 by the death of the Duke of Lauderdale. In his place James, Duke of York (afterwards James VII and II), was appointed Commissioner for Scotland, a position in which he won considerable popularity. He made no secret of being a Roman Catholic and when the Scots Parliament passed a Test Act, the immediate royal family were excepted from it. This Act did, however, catch the Earl of Argyll and resulted in his being found guilty of high treason in 1681. He was imprisoned in Edinburgh Castle but was allowed to escape and fled abroad. A few years later he was to lead an unsuccessful rebellion against James II. The House of Campbell supported by Lauderdale had reverted to all its old ways. 'The Campbell empire now included Mull, Morvern and Tilee, and there were many discontented chieftains ready to fall upon Argyll when Lauderdale's protected died.' (Mitchison, *History of Scotland*, p 267.)

As Commissioner for Scotland, James was particularly well-liked by the Highlanders with whom he treated as Monk had done, through their chiefs. Many of them were to rise enthusiastically for him in his hour of need.

In the Lowlands, John Graham of Claverhouse pursued a policy of force, but nowhere near as bloody as subsequent writing by his enemies has represented it to be. He was a distant kinsman of the great Montrose, the common line of descent being traceable to about 1400, when Sir William Graham had several sons, ancestors of the numerous Graham lines.

Thus, with consideration for their ancient traditions, some measure of tranquillity existed in the Highlands until the accession of James, Duke of York, to the thrones of England and Scotland brought calamity to the adherents of the Stuarts.

H

8 The Age of Revolution

CHARLES II DIED ON 6 February 1685 and without delay or difficulty his brother James II succeeded him. At first James was very popular. He was a good admiral who had done much for the Navy, and he had shown that he was brave in action. He had also been successful as Commissioner in Scotland. When he was crowned on St George's Day, 23 April 1685, he was, in the customary formula used by the Archbishop of Canterbury on the occasion of a coronation, the undoubted sovereign of the three kingdoms.[1] Some discontented persons there were, mainly exiles in Holland. Two of them, the Earl of Argyll and the Duke of Monmouth, a bastard of the late King's, prepared expeditions for the invasion of Britain. With Monmouth's, which was launched in Dorset on 11 June, we have no concern, but it was remarkable for seeing the last full-scale battle fought on English soil, that of Sedgemoor on 6 July 1685. The rebellion was crushed and Monmouth, after an abject and vain appeal to his uncle for mercy, was beheaded on 15 July.

Argyll's attempt began earlier than Monmouth's. He left Holland on 2 May 1685 with three ships and 300 men. On 6 May this force reached Cairston, in the Orkneys, and about a week later Argyll landed on the mainland at Kintyre. The fiery cross was sent round to call in Argyll's clansmen and vassals. Having gathered about 2,500 men, he invaded the Lowlands where some of his army deserted him, and he abandoned the rest. Argyll was soon captured and again imprisoned in Edinburgh. The sentence of death for high treason passed upon him in 1681 still stood, so there was no need of a new trial. Accordingly, he was embraced by the Maiden as his father had been, and with the fall of his head under the knife there ended a life of tortuous and ineffectual intrigue.

Not only was James VII of Scotland and James II of England and Ireland the undoubted sovereign of these realms, but those unprincipled persons who had rebelled against him had, within a matter of weeks, paid the penalty with their lives.

So it might have continued and the House of Stuart have reigned over Britain in perpetuity. However, James's desire to become an absolute monarch and to make his subjects once more adherents to the Church of Rome had within three years turned loyalty and adulation into conspiracy and rebellion. A focus of disloyalty and intrigue existed in Holland, in the court of the Prince of Orange, James's son-in-law, who was married to his eldest surviving daughter. William of Orange coveted the throne of England, not so much for itself as for the great increase in power which it would give him in the struggle that he was preparing against Louis XIV of France. A cold, phlegmatic man, William estimated correctly the motives of the noble conspirators who came to him from England and Scotland. They did not love him but thought that, under a foreign sovereign who owed his throne to them, they would be able to do as they liked, instead of having to submit to the rigorous control of a legitimate and absolute sovereign.

In Scotland the regime of King James was peaceful. The clansmen had supported him against Argyll and when the threat of William's descent became known the Scottish Privy Council called upon the chiefs to have their clans ready under arms and proposed that an army of 13,000 men, part militia and part Highlanders, should be formed and sent to the Borders ready to march into England in support of James. The King declined this proposal and asked instead for the support of the small Scots regular army of some 3,000 men. The Council's suggestion, however, shows the confidence they felt in the loyalty and trustworthiness of the Highlanders. To the minds of the chiefs and their principal clansmen the idea of a Dutch prince taking the place of the King of Scots, their Chief of Chiefs, must have seemed most incongruous, especially as they had had no say in the matter.

All James's actions after William had landed at Torbay were ill advised and in the latter part of December William's cunning manoeuvres induced him to leave England. It was not hard to make his disappearance from the country look like abandonment of his crown and though he never, in fact, did so, he was held to have abdicated and William and Mary were crowned in his place. Even in England the new king, William III, was not popular. Everyone knew that he had been brought in to replace his father-in-law only to secure the Protestant succession. James, for his part, took refuge in France but soon invaded Ireland, where the whole country with the exception of two cities went over to him. In the Highlands of Scotland the pro-Stuart feeling was strong and the man to direct it was John Graham of Claverhouse. He was forty-five years of age when James lost his throne. He had had experience of war on the Continent and in Scotland at Drumclog and Bothwell bridge, and afterwards had hunted down the Covenanting sectaries with perseverance and skill. He was greatly advanced by Charles II, being made a Sheriff of Wigtown in 1682, a Privy Councillor in 1684, a captain of the Royal Regiment of Horse and given the estate of Dudhope and the constabularyship of Dundee. King James promoted him to the rank of brigadier, and then major-general, and raised him to the peerage as Viscount of Dundee and Lord Graham of Claverhouse on 12 November 1688, seven days after the landing of William of Orange.

William's adherents knew that the bulk of the Highlanders and the episcopalians of the north were opposed to him. They had a lively memory of the Highlanders' exploits under the leadership of Montrose and dreaded what might happen with another brilliant soldier to lead the clansmen. It was also known that, apart from their loyalty to the Stuarts, many chiefs were afraid of the return of the new Earl of Argyll, realising that if he should hold high place again there would be harsh treatment of his debtors among the clansmen. The amount outstanding was estimated by Argyll at £5,000 and, to forestall trouble, the Government made an offer to the chiefs to repay it, and at the same time made a separate proposition to the chief of the Macleans for settlement of the difficulties he had had with the late earl.

The commander of the Government forces was General Hugh Mackay of Scowry, a very experienced professional soldier who had served in the armies of France, Venice and Holland. He had been invited to England by James II in 1685 and appointed as major-general in command of the forces in Scotland. However, in 1686 he resigned his commission as he did not agree with James's proceedings and returned to Holland. Here William of Orange commissioned him as major-general and after accompanying him to England he was appointed commander of all the forces in Scotland on 4 January 1689.

It was this General Mackay who now tried to discuss the Government's offer of £5,000 in settlement of debt with Cameron of Lochiel, from whom he received no reply, and with Macdonell of Glengarry. Glengarry viewed it as a bribe to ensure his quietude and sarcastically suggested that Mackay should imitate General Monk and march to restore the legitimate sovereign. Perhaps one of the reasons why the chiefs refused this offer of cash was that the negotiator in the business was to be Campbell of Cawdor. He is said to have been *persona non grata* to the chiefs, and in any event a Campbell's judgement as regards the rights of his chiefs was hardly likely to be unbiased.

Moreover, the arguments advanced by the Whig politicians of the day, well represented by Mackay in his appeals to the chiefs, were hardly calculated to interest them; appeals to Protestant feelings against the Papist James, contentions that he had by his actions renounced his crown; further arguments on behalf of William of Orange that he was a defender of liberty and an excellent king and so on, carried no weight in the Highlands where James was seen as a good king by right divine and one who had come nearest to fulfilling his grandfather's (James VI's) ideal of kingship.[2] In England, too, James had proved, before succeeding to the throne, a good administrator, especially as regards the armed forces, and, ironically enough, the Royal Navy later demonstrated the value of his reforms in their defeat of the French at La Hogue. James was a patriot then, as he had been at the battle of the Dunes years previously, in applauding the action of the English fighting men though directed against himself.

Mackay's efforts to bring over the chiefs failed except in a few instances, and those the least martial of the clansmen. Lord Murray for one brought only about 200 of the Atholl men to Mackay's aid, the bulk going to Dundee.

Meanwhile, Dundee was in the Highlands successfully raising an army. Like all leaders of the clans he found his greatest trials not with the enemy but with his own men. A long campaign was not the Highlanders' idea of war, although in their marches to Worcester and to Derby they showed that they could endure protracted warfare. Their ideal was a good swift fight, a collection of booty and a speedy return home. Consequently a commander might go to his tent at night knowing that three to four thousand warriors were in the camp, and the next morning at muster would find that half had gone.

Dundee, like Mackay, was a professional soldier who had served in France and Holland prior to his operations against the Whig Covenanters from 1679 onwards. He did suggest to the chiefs who followed him in 1689 that they should try to imbue the Highlanders with some semblance of military discipline, but they assured him that it would be useless to attempt it and Dundee wisely decided to let the Highlanders fight in their own fashion.

Though Mackay was a Highlander, he had long been absent from Scotland in the course of his duties as a professional soldier, and he now failed to understand or win over the clansmen. Dundee, on the other hand, was a Lowlander, and as Montrose had shown, only a distinguished man who was not a Highlander could hope to bring any number of the clans together under his leadership. The chiefs would never have agreed to the appointment of one of their own number as commander-in-chief. A modern parallel is the extraordinary skill of an Englishman, Colonel T. E. Lawrence, in leading some of the tribes in Arabia. He, likewise, had the problem caused by departure of tribesmen after battle, taking home their plunder.

Much marching and counter-marching ensued between the two generals and their forces. Each commander had his special difficulties; Mackay's lay in the wild nature of the country and his failure to obtain many Highland auxiliaries, while Dundee was let down when King James's promise of substantial reinforcements from Ireland produced only 300 badly equipped and half-trained Irish troops.

At length Mackay, in response to an urgent request from Lord Murray, left Perth and marched towards Dunkeld. His army was then of about 4,500 men, a largish proportion being cavalry. The intelligence which he had from Murray was that Dundee was marching rapidly through Badenoch to relieve Blair Castle (Blair Atholl), 35 miles from Perth at the junction of the Tilt and Garry rivers, which Murray's forces were blockading. If Dundee got to Blair Atholl he could probably secure the whole district, which would mean a further accession to his forces by the Highlanders. On the night of 26 July 1689, while Mackay's army camped at Dunkeld, news came from Murray that Dundee had reached Atholl and that he had been obliged to lift the blockade of Blair Castle as most of his men had deserted him. They drank a health to King James from the water of a burn, but did not all join Dundee; instead, a number posted themselves in the heights above the pass of Killiecrankie where they would be well placed to fall upon any fugitives. In his message to Mackay, Murray added that he had put a guard at the end of the famous pass nearest to Dundee's army, his object being to enable Mackay to get his army through the pass in order to confront Dundee.

At daybreak on 27 July Mackay marched towards Killiecrankie, reaching the entrance about 10 o'clock in the morning. Those who have been taken through the pass, perhaps on an archaeological tour, will have to exercise their imagination to realise what it was like 300 years ago. No road then existed, only a track over which a wheeled carriage had never been taken.

On reaching the pass, Mackay sent forward 200 men under Lieutenant-Colonel Lauder to secure the exit. They found none of Lord Murray's men, though he later turned up with the two to three hundred, the remnants of his force. Mackay gave his men two hours' rest and then sent them through the pass, described by one historian as 'a frightful chasm, out of which they might possibly never return'.[3] Another writer describes the passage: 'Even the foot had to climb by twos and threes; and the baggage horses 1,200 in number, could mount only one at a time.' During the passage, Mackay was undisturbed by his opponent, except that one of the cavalry was shot by a man named Ian Ban Beg MacRon, who was probably fighting for his own hand. Dundee had now reached Blair Castle and only then learned that Mackay was approaching the pass. Had he been able to get there in time, Dundee would surely have attacked Mackay's army as it toiled through the pass.

The Government troops got through the passage and debouched on to some flat ground in a small valley with the river Garry on their left and some rising ground on their right. They rested for a few hours until, in the early afternoon, a Highland force appeared on the top of a hill in their front.

The numbers of the forces were approximately 2,000–3,000 for Dundee; 4,000–4,500 for Mackay, but the latter had a much higher proportion of trained soldiers. Mackay drew up his men with every battalion divided into two parts, and with the intention of fighting in three ranks. The cavalry were posted in rear in order to attack the Highlanders in flank. He also felt that, as some of the cavalry were recently raised units, it would be unwise to expose them to attack by Dundee's more experienced troopers.

At the appearance of the Highlanders, Mackay's troops had at once been alerted and the two armies faced each other until the early evening. With Dundee were the Macleans, the Macdonalds of Clanranald, and other branches of Clan Donald, the Camerons and the men of Skye led by Macdonald of Sleat. Apart from some desultory fire and the occasional fall of a clansman, there was no action until about 7 o'clock.

Mackay's army was in a very dangerous position. To advance uphill against the enemy was inadvisable and he therefore awaited their attack, knowing they were delaying it until, with the coming of the night, they could assail him with demoralising effect. Mackay's troops, too, must have been partially aware of their precarious position.

At last the Highland army began to advance. In their customary fashion, the men stripped off their plaids and gradually quickened their pace until, at a short distance from the enemy, they discharged their firearms, threw them down and with a mighty shout rushed headlong against Mackay's line. The troops were ordered to fix bayonets to receive the clansmen, but these were the days before bayonets were screwed on to muskets[4] and while Mackay's men were still trying to push them into the muzzles—which, of course, prevented them from firing another round—the Highlanders burst upon them like a fighting flood. There was little resistance, Mackay's main lines gave way and were swept off the field. Most of his cavalry fled, and the General was in danger of being left almost alone when he noticed a small body of his men on the right, including some of Hasting's English Regiment, who were unbroken. They had continued to pour a steady fire into the Highlanders and to keep them off with their pikes. Joining this small contingent and collecting any other remnants of his forces, Mackay retreated across the Garry in an endeavour to escape from the pursuit which he thought to be inevitable. He did not know that after their first tremendous rush the clansmen had fallen upon his baggage train and were far too busy plundering it. Nor did he know something even more important. His victorious opponent, Dundee, had been shot and had died soon afterwards. A Covenanting superstition had it that 'Bloody Clavers' bore a charmed life and that only a silver bullet, specially made, could kill one whom the Covenanters regarded as being under Satan's protection. Whatever the nature of the bullet, its work was done and the mainspring of the Highland Host was broken.

Unaware that no pursuit was being attempted by the clansmen, Mackay struggled on, falling in on his way with bodies of utterly demoralised men from his army, more like collections of fugitives than detachments of soldiers. In that wild Highland country Mackay had the greatest difficulty in finding his way, but fortunately for his defeated remnant he still remembered the Gaelic he had spoken in his youth and was able to question cottagers he encountered. With their aid and that of a rough map, he was able to extricate his following from the wilderness and to reach Castle Weems, near Aberfeldy. On the following day he marched towards Stirling, and on the way about one hundred of his men fled into the countryside on an alarm of the approach of Highlanders. These runaways were mostly killed and stripped of their belongings by the inhabitants of the district.

The defeated general reached Stirling on 28 July, and on the same day the news was heard at Edinburgh where the utmost consternation was felt, and even responsible observers thought that the country north of the Forth would have temporarily to be given up to the followers of Dundee.

Most of Mackay's army had gone; out of some 4,000 he succeeded in bringing back not more than 400. Vast numbers were killed on the battlefield. One narrator wrote: 'I dare be bold to say, that were scarce ever such strokes given in Europe as were given that day by the Highlanders. Many of General Mackay's officers and soldiers were cut down through the skull and neck to the very breast; others had skulls cut off above their ears like night caps, some soldiers had both their bodies and cross belts cut through at one blow; pikes and small swords were cut like willows.'[5] Not since their battles with the Mongols and the Turks had European armies had to encounter such fierce adversaries. At the same time the loss of some 900 of the clansmen showed that well-aimed fire could accomplish much. Had it been directed with the skill shown at Culloden, the Highland army might have lost half its number.

At the same time, the weakness of the clan forces was shown most vividly by Killiecrankie. A brilliant victory, it yet accomplished nothing. There was no pursuit, and Mackay was able to gather a fresh army. The Highlanders were so intent on collecting spoils that they allowed the fugitives to escape. Above all, the general was gone and there was no one to take his place. Colonel Cannon assumed command on Dundee's death but, although an experienced soldier, he knew nothing about the Highlanders. Joined by the Stuarts of Appin and the Macgregors, he advanced to Dunkeld, sixteen miles from Killiecrankie, but a party of 300 of the Atholl men whom he sent to Perth were completely routed with heavy loss by Mackay's cavalry. Cannon then retreated northward, followed by Mackay who had got together a force of some 1,500 men. Mackay asked for reinforcements and among the Government troops ordered forward was the Earl of Angus's, or Cameronian Regiment which consisted of the stern religious fanatics from the western Lowlands. They were now on the Government side and bitterly opposed to any who had followed the late 'Bloody Clavers'. As Mackay did not want them with him, thinking that they would be intensely hated in the northern counties, they were stationed at Dunkeld and their importance in this history arises from the successful stand they made against the Highlanders.

News now came through that the Highlanders were marching on Dunkeld, and the Cameronians entrenched themselves in some enclosures around the Marquess of Atholl's mansion there. Colonel Cleland, their commander, posted some of his men in the cathedral tower and other places of vantage and when the Highlanders attacked furiously, they were met by as furious a fire and most determined resistance. The firing continued for three hours and the losses of the Highlanders were far greater than those of the Cameronians. Colonel Cleland was one of the few Cameronians killed, but his successor, Captain Munro, was equally resolute. He decided to drive the Highlanders out of the town by setting it on fire. Small parties of the Cameronians went into the town with burning faggots on the points of their pikes, Dunkeld was set on fire and sixteen Highlanders were burnt to death in one house alone. Their total losses in this action were 300 and they refused to attack the Cameronians again. A Lowland regiment had defeated the Highlanders.

Blaming their defeat on Colonel Cannon's incapacity, the chiefs returned to their glens but agreed to continue fighting for King James and in the defence of their homes. Mackay, meanwhile, rebuilt the old Cromwellian fort at Inverlochy, which he renamed Fort William. There were still alarums and excursions on the part of the Jacobites, but by 1 July 1690 the Battle of the Boyne had ended James II's Irish adventure and most of his hopes in Scotland. The chiefs applied to King James for his permission to agree to a pacification. James II gave them permission to make the best terms they could with the Government, which, on 27 August 1691, issued a proclamation promising indemnity to all persons who had been in arms against King William and who should take an oath of allegiance to the Government before 1 January 1692.

James II had consented to the chiefs parleying with the Government because there was nothing else that he could do. Both in Ireland and in Scotland his military plans had gone wrong. Even had they been successful, so long as England had remained loyal to William III the Jacobite cause could not have succeeded. An England solid behind William of Orange, as in effect it had been behind Cromwell, would inevitably have recovered control of Scotland and Ireland.

From 1689 it is reasonable to refer to the supporters of the exiled Stuarts as Jacobites, and from this date comes the famous and romantic phrase, 'the King across the water'. Ardent Jacobites would toast their exiled king as they passed the glass over a bowl of water, a gesture which could be made even in company where differing political views existed. For nearly a century Jacobitism existed, but with declining power until at last it faded away, even before the death of Prince Charles Edward.

Two hopes as elusive as the proverbial rainbow's end dangled before the imagination of the Jacobites; a great rising of English Jacobites and a substantial landing of French troops. It was always assumed that the Highlanders or the Irish must rise first to trigger off the rebellion of the slower moving English; but it was also strongly felt that French assistance would be needed, not only in money and supplies but in the form of a large body of regular troops. To some observers this linking of Scots and French may have seemed like a renewal of the Auld Alliance, which had been terminated in the sixteenth century when the Scots left Catholicism for Protestantism. This lined them up with their English co-religionists and for the first time in 300 years the Scots began to like their southern neighbours, and even expressed gratitude for them in their prayers.[6] Whatever the Highlanders might think, the great bulk of the Scots, those in the Lowlands, were anti-Jacobite.

The employment of French or other foreign troops—a few hundred Spaniards got past the Royal Navy in 1719—was fatal in English eyes to the cause of the Stuarts, as had been the case in the sixteenth century when the efforts of the Jesuits and other Catholic priests to bring the English back to Catholicism were fatally handicapped by final reliance on Spanish aid. When the Armada threatened England, the whole country rallied behind Queen Elizabeth, Catholics along with Protestants. So with the Jacobites' threat. If it had to depend on a foreign power, and a Catholic one at that, the Jacobite cause had no hope of success in England or Lowland Scotland.

Ireland, after the Boyne and the Treaty of Limerick, was lost to the Stuarts. The Vinegar Hill rising in 1798 had nothing to do with Jacobitism; emphatically it was a matter of Irish nationalism, 'ourselves alone'. As for England, after Cromwell's time the Cavaliers did almost nothing for the Stuarts except for the abortive northern rally in 1715 and the provision of 200–300 men under Francis Townley in the '45.

The Highlanders, then, were left to 'go it alone', and their fortunes declined along with those of their former kings. A government quite indifferent to their interests now ruled from London; and another government in Edinburgh regarded them as fit objects for hatred and deliberate genocide. *Mi-run mor nan Gall*[7]—the Highlanders' description of the Lowlanders' intense hatred for the Gael–had grown greater with each generation.

William III could hardly be expected to take any interest in Highland clans. He was more concerned with preparing for the coming struggle against France and naturally tended to see Highland affairs as his Scottish advisers presented them to him. In the aftermath of the Killiecrankie campaign, the main object of the Scottish Government was to render the clans innocuous. Cajolery and force, in the form of money bribes and letters of fire and sword, both of the old methods, were again brought out for use. A great new fort, named after William III, was erected at Inverlochy and a strong garrison stationed there. The 1st Earl of Breadalbane, and Viscount Tarbat, later 1st Earl of Cromartie, were both engaged in devious negotiations with the chiefs. Breadalbane, as a Campbell, was almost automatically suspected of bad faith by the clansmen. Tarbat represented himself to the chiefs as being really a Jacobite (he did actually come out for King James in 1715, two years before he died), and to the Government as a staunch supporter of King William. Not surprisingly, Tarbat's mission was a failure and the imputation that he had made off with money which had been provided to pay the chiefs was widely believed. The sum, about £10,000, was supposed to be paid for buying up the superiorities of the chiefs' lands, a recurrent cause of trouble in the Highlands. Tarbat did not embezzle it, but his way of accounting for its disbursement was open to suspicion. When asked by Lord Nottingham to account for it, he replied: 'The money is spent, the Highlands are quiet, and this is the only way of accounting among friends.'[8]

For the rest of William's reign (up to 1702) the Highlands were quiet, and not only because most of the chiefs came in and took the oath of allegiance, with or without the 'bonny English siller'. But before they settled down to a decade of comparative quietude, there was one more example of the real attitude of the Scottish Government towards the Highlanders. This was the famous, or infamous, Massacre of Glencoe.[9]

When the Government had offered the chiefs indemnity for past offences in return for taking an oath of loyalty to William, it was stated that the offer was open to 1 January 1692. Those who did not come in by that time were threatened with the utmost extremity of the law. The principal Scottish adviser of the King at this time was John Dalrymple, Master of Stair, and son of Viscount Stair, who subsequently became the 1st Earl of Stair. In December 1691 he was Secretary of State for Scotland, having previously been Lord Justice Clark and Lord Advocate.

The period of the year by which the chiefs must come in was that of the worst weather. Deep snow lay on all the tracks and the sea separating the western isles from the mainland was tempestuous. Some chiefs simply could not get in. 'Clanranald was not merely late in taking the oath, but never did take it. He was a minor with influential friends and took refuge in France, while his clansmen and estates were left unmolested till he returned to them peacefully in Queen Anne's time.' (Cunningham, op cit, p 407.) Similar leniency was extended to Sir John Maclean. The MacDonald of Glencoe, however, had no such influential friends, only very influential enemies, among them the Earl of Breadalbane and the Master of Stair, the latter being in a key position to injure Glencoe. Like the Macgregors, the Macdonalds or Macians of Glencoe had built up for themselves an evil reputation and were referred to in Stair's correspondence as a set of thieves. They had a long tradition of violence, of which the following incidents are samples. They fought in Montrose's army and, as so often happened with the clans, took the opportunity to settle scores with old enemies. Along with their kinsfolk of Keppoch, they had raided Breadalbane in December 1645 on their way home from the war. Another raid in June 1646 by Glencoe and Keppoch left thirty-six Campbells dead in Breadalbane. There was a third raid on Breadalbane and on Glen Lyon in 1655. In 1674 MacIan, the chief, was held prisoner in Edinburgh on a charge of killing several Macdonalds, but he escaped. In 1685, when Argyll's rising failed, the Glencoe men were more or less legitimately able to ravage Kilbride, Cowal and Rosneath. Again in 1689, on the way home from Killiecrankie, Glencoe and Keppoch went through Glen Lyon very thoroughly.

A series of incidents of this nature soon builds up into a situation where a smouldering resentment can find expression under the guise of carrying out a national duty. Government policy being in favour of making an example of a clan or two, *pour encourager les autres*, the choice would easily be narrowed down to a particular sept which was friendless and the object of malice and revenge by powerful enemies. William III was a cold, hard man, quite willing to take the profits of a murder without actually planning or executing it, and he did not require much persuasion from Stair to agree to what was planned, although, for reasons of State, the subsequent commission exonerated him of responsiblity for what happened.

The oath had to be taken before the sheriff of the county. Sir Ewen Cameron of Lochiel, hardly likely to be among the earliest to submit, went to Inverary on 30 December and so was inside the limit. He probably sent word to Glencoe urging the need for haste in complying with the conditions. Keppoch had already come in.

Alastair MacDonald of Glencoe was about sixty years of age, a huge man 6ft 7in in height and powerful in proportion. He had been educated in Paris and was the twelfth chief of his line. Knowing the number of his enemies and perhaps fearing to put himself in the hands of the authorities even for a short while, he yet set out to swear the detested oath but, instead of going to Inverary, he went up to Fort William, whose English governor, Colonel Hill, had been an officer in Cromwell's army and had known Glencoe in his youth. It was 30/31 December, and Glencoe had arrived at the wrong place. Hill could not administer the oath, and Glencoe must go to the Sheriff at Inverary. The Sheriff was Campbell of Ardkinglas. Glencoe was reluctant to swear before a Campbell but was persuaded by Hill, who wrote a letter to Ardkinglas asking that Glencoe be received as a lost sheep. Travelling on through the winter weather, the chief reached Inverary on 2 January. The Sheriff was away and he was unable to take the oath until 5/6 January, when Ardkinglas returned.

Lost indeed was Glencoe. Five weeks later, at 5 am on the morning of 13 February 1692, an attack was made on the Macdonalds of Glencoe. The chief was shot and killed as he was getting out of bed. His last words were to a servant, ordering him to get a dram for the young officer who was about to kill him, for Glencoe thought the officer had come to bid him farewell. The houses of the clan were burnt, their cattle stolen, and their belongings plundered; thirty-eight of the people were killed, about one-tenth of the total clan number. The rest escaped over the hills despite the severity of the weather on which their enemies had counted for getting them into the trap.

It was not the numbers killed which evoked horror all over the Highlands and in England, for time and again many more Highlanders had been slain in foray and clan conflict. They had, however, been killed in hot blood and fair fight whereas the Macdonalds had been attacked by their guests in grossest breach of the sacred law of hospitality. Not even by a technicality could the Government be absolved from complicity. Granted that Glencoe was five days late in taking the oath, yet he had taken it and no one had said that he had failed to keep the conditions. No one at Inverary. But in London, and more so in Edinburgh, there had been dark plotters weaving a scheme of horrible intent. It had been hoped that Keppoch and Glencoe would not come in within the limits allowed and Stair is said to have expressed regret when he heard that Glencoe had taken the oath. When it became known that the oath-taking was five days late, Stair rejoiced: 'It would', he said, 'be a great work of charity to proceed against Glencoe in rooting out that damnable sept.' The King's orders to Sir Thomas Livingstone, C-in-C Scotland, were that he should cut off the obstinate rebels.

Two companies of Argyll's regiment under Captain Robert Campbell of Glenlyon marched to Glencoe and requested shelter until they could proceed allegedly (though falsely) to punish Macdonnell of Glengarry, another chief who had been late in taking the oath. No harm, he assured the Macdonalds, was intended and he offered his parole of honour. Hospitality was given and despite the long-standing enmity between Campbell and Macdonald, the soldiers were received as guests and made welcome. This was on 1 February. On 12 February, Major Robert Duncanson of Fassorie sent orders to Glenlyon to begin the massacre at 5 am on 13 February, none under the age of seventy to be spared. Glenlyon was too heavy a drinker to be an efficient commander and, through his failure to blockade the exits, most of the Glencoe Macdonalds escaped, though many of the older folk and the children later died in the mountains from hardship and exhaustion.

Public outcry against the horror of the massacre resulted in the appointment of a commission in 1693 which proved quite useless, and of another in 1695 which did little better. No one was punished for his share in the murders, and though it was recommended that the Macdonalds should be allowed to return to their homes and be given compensation for their losses, the second part of the recommendation does not appear to have been carried out.

What was the effect of the massacre on the other clans during the rest of King William's reign? Did the principle, *oderint dum metuant* really operate? Since there were no further risings, the country could be said to have been quiet, but an account of the career of Simon Fraser, who eventually assumed the title of 11th Baron Lovat, proves how little respect there was for law. This man, born in the early 1670s, was the effective head of the Fraser clan and was always ready to call them to arms in his support. Time and again he managed to defy the law and on one occasion, having failed to elope with the heiress of the family, he raped the mother in a forced marriage. In consequence of yet other activities he was tried in absence in 1698 and found guilty of treason. In the following year he assumed the title of Lovat and lived by pillage and robbery until, through Argyll's good offices, he secured a pardon for his offences, except the rape. On this account he was outlawed and fled to France in 1702, to serve King James. In 1715, he earned remission of his previous sentence by turning pro-Government and even secured legal recognition of his title. Eventually he made the grave mistake of being a Jacobite in the '45 and, having been found guilty of high treason, his head fell from the block on Tower Hill on 9 April 1747.

Thus, for several centuries the Scottish Government had followed alternative policies of force and of bribery towards the clans. As it never had enough force to subdue the Highlands, it had to resort to playing one clan off against another, but the numbers never diminished, nor during that period did the Highlands become truly peaceful.

I

9 The 1715 Rebellion

THE REIGN OF Queen Anne was like an interval between two periods of violent struggle. In 1701, the year just previous to Anne's accession, James II died at St Germains. Louis XIV had been the most kind of hosts to the fallen sovereign and when James besought his help for his son, the thirteen-year-old Prince of Wales, Louis promised the dying man that he would look after the young James. Accordingly, when James II was dead, Louis recognised his son as James VIII and III King of England, Scotland and Ireland. The Treaty of Ryswick in 1697 had, however, established what was virtually a truce between Louis and William III, and William protested that Louis' action was in breach of that treaty. Hostilities between England and France did not immediately begin, and matters were further postponed by William's death in 1702.

He was succeeded by his sister-in-law, Anne (half-sister of James VIII) who was married to Prince George of Denmark. They had had numerous children, but when the only surviving child, the Duke of Gloucester, died at the age of eleven in 1700, it was felt that Anne's reign would, at best, be only the prelude to the restoration of her half-brother, known as James VIII and III to his adherents and in Government circles as the Pretender to the British throne.

The failure of the Darian colonisation scheme in 1695-7 had caused immense bitterness in Scotland, as the English were held responsible for it, and at the height of this ill feeling against England the Scots Parliament passed two Acts (in 1703 and 1704)[1] which then envisaged the possibility, on the death of Queen Anne, of a sovereign being chosen in Scotland different from the sovereign in England. The thought that, after a century of union of the Crowns, they might once again be

disunited greatly troubled the English leaders, and their
anxieties were increased by the reflection that a completely
independent Scotland might be ruled by a Catholic Stuart—
an unlikely happening, at best, in a predominantly Protestant
and Presbyterian country. By the Act of Settlement in 1701,[2]
the English Parliament had already determined that the Crown
should pass to the descendants of Princess Elizabeth, the
daughter of James VI and I. Elizabeth had been the 'winter
Queen' of Bohemia, married to Frederick V, the Elector Pala-
tine. Elizabeth's daughter was Sophia, who married Ernest
Augustus, Elector of Hanover.[3] Elizabeth had had other children but the Electoral Prince and his wife were Protestants and
all other persons descended from the Stuarts, to the number,
then, of fifty-three, were excluded from the succession as being
Catholics. The succession to the English throne had to be
limited to Protestants. Never again would the liberties of the
country be endangered by a Catholic sovereign. It had been
the birth of a male heir to James II which had precipitated the
Glorious Revolution in 1688. James's Catholicism could be
tolerated for his lifetime perhaps, knowing that his two Protestant daughters were waiting in line of succession to him, but
a son of James meant the prospect of a line of Catholic princes.
Hence not only the Revolution but the cruel story of the warming-pan Prince of Wales. (The story, believed in some anti-
Stuart circles, was that the Old Pretender was not a Stuart at
all but a child smuggled into the palace in a warming-pan.)

The Act of 1701 was entitled 'An Act for the further limita-
tion of the Crown and better securing the rights and liberties
of the subject'. The two things were felt to stand or fall together. In the sequel, the Electress Sophia never wore the
Crown Imperial, as she predeceased Queen Anne and a heavy
German prince came over to be crowned as George I.

This is to anticipate, for with the passing of the Scots Act
of 1703 those who favoured union of the two countries felt
that the moment of decision had come. Full union between
England and Scotland, union of the parliaments and economic
union, not merely a union of the Crowns, was the goal of a
few on both sides of the Border. The idea was not popular in
either country; perhaps truer to say that it was unpopular in
England and most unpopular in Scotland. The Earl of Stair

came out of the retirement into which he had tactfully withdrawn after Glencoe and used all his powers of persuasion to make the scheme of union succeed. He died in his sleep on 7/8 January 1707, and the Act of Union was passed on 16 January that year.[4]

It continued to be most disliked in Scotland and then, if ever, the arrival of the Stuart prince could have been expected to serve as focus point for the national feeling. In the early months of 1707 Louis XIV sent an agent named Hooke to sound opinion in Scotland and see if a French force landed in aid of the Pretender could count on native support. Hooke returned in May with a very sanguine report and preparations were made for a French army to assemble at Dunkirk, with a fleet to transport it to Scotland.

In England, measures were taken to combat the threatened invasion. Habeus corpus was suspended and both Houses of Parliament passed resolutions to defend the Queen against the 'pretended Prince of Wales'. A large fleet was sent to cruise off Dunkirk but stress of weather dispersed it, and the French men-of-war, with troopships carrying over 5,000 men, set sail. The Pretender was with them, carrying with him many rich gifts from Louis XIV, including a sword studded with diamonds. Jacobite agents had been sent ahead and landed in Scotland to prepare for the arrival of the French. The French fleet reached the Firth of Forth on 23 March 1708. Next morning a strong British fleet appeared, standing in to the Forth. Immediately the French admiral, seeking safety, sailed northward, and later, threatened by storms, the whole expedition returned to Dunkirk, having lost one vessel to the Royal Navy. The Pretender showed courage and pleaded with the French commander to put him ashore, even if he were accompanied only by his servants.[5]

Thus, one of the attempts for a Stuart restoration which might have succeeded, failed dismally, and the Government later arrested all persons suspected of Jacobitism. The clans were never afoot. Indeed, the Government had passed a Bill which released them from their vassalage to any chief who rose in arms against Queen Anne, but as the clansmen were unlikely to have understood this measure, it was of doubtful value and the matter never came to the test.

In contemplating the 1708 attempt to restore the Pretender, it is hard to realise that at the same time England (after 1707, Britain) was engaged in a serious continental war which had its repercussions in India and America. During the period of Marlborough's triumphs at Blenheim, Ramillies, Oudenarde and Malplaquet; and while Pope, Swift, Addison and Steele were giving to the reign of Anne an Augustan literary quality, at this same time Jacobites were intriguing and using every possible means to overthrow the Government. The French participation was perfectly understandable. If by landing troops in Britain, they could encourage a rebellion, a useful distraction to the British would be created and the Government might be compelled to recall troops from Flanders, as indeed had to be done in 1745.

The attempt of 1708, like later attempts, failed because of the Royal Navy's control of the sea, but the French never applied their full force to the restoration of the Stuarts. Despite Louis XIV's promise to the dying James II, his and his successors' efforts never approached those by which the British in the next century thrust the Bourbons back on France.

In 1710 the Whigs were driven from office by Tory intrigue, especially by their harping on the cost of Marlborough's campaigns, and as a result of the Treaty of Utrecht in 1713, Louis XIV escaped total ruin in the invasion of France which Marlborough was preparing. The leading Tory ministers were Harley, Earl of Oxford, and Henry St John, Viscount Bolingbroke. They headed two factions and thus divided their party, whereas the Whigs were united and ready to take a German prince as King, provided he guaranteed the Protestant succession and the liberties of England. The question 'Whether the Protestant succession is in danger under the present administration?' was actually asked in the House of Lords, whereupon the Duke of Argyll offered to prove that the Lord Treasurer, the Earl of Oxford, had sent annual sums to the Highland chiefs who favoured the Stuarts. (The head of the house of Campbell had more than recovered his position after William of Orange became William III, and in 1701 had been created Duke of Argyll along with the gift of four other peerages. He died in 1703, and his son, the 2nd Duke, was the speaker in the Lords mentioned above.)[6]

The answer given by Oxford was that he was merely carrying on the policy of William III towards the clans, but shortly afterwards he was removed from the Treasuryship. The Jacobites hoped that Bolingbroke would succeed him, but the Tories were soon out of office following upon the death of the Queen on 1 August 1714. As Professor Feiling wrote: 'Stocks in the London money-market rose cheerfully, for the Queen had died early that morning and the nightmare of civil war faded away. Under the Act of 1705 power automatically passed from Bolingbroke's Cabinet to Lords Justices chosen by the new King, all Whigs save the enigmatic Duke of Shrewsbury and the Hanoverian Tories, Anglesey and Nottingham.' (*The Second Tory Party, 1714–1832*, 1959, p 13.)

George knew no English, and little about the country, but he did know that he had to thank the Tories for bringing the Allies' victories in the War of the Spanish Succession to an end and in involving his family in serious loss.

On the same day that the Queen died the lords of the Privy Council issued a proclamation to the effect that the imperial crowns of Britain, France and Ireland 'had solely and rightfully come to the high and mighty Prince George, Elector of Brunswick Lenenburg'. Proclaimed by the English heralds on 1 August, George I was likewise proclaimed on 5 August at the Mercat Cross, Edinburgh by the Lord Lyon. He was crowned on 20 October 1714, so that no time was lost in establishing his position.

Thus unity and single-mindedness of purpose on the part of the Whigs set on the throne the dynasty which still occupies it. By contrast, the weakness and infirmity of purpose of the Jacobites effectually precluded any hopes of the Pretender's return. Queen Anne had had a sentimental attachment to the half-brother she had never seen, but she was a constitutional sovereign bound by the Acts of Parliament which she had signed. It is just conceivable that a vigorous and united Tory party could have brought about James's accession, and, indeed, Francis Atterbury, Bishop of Rochester, offered to proclaim him at Charing Cross. When his proposal was rejected he exclaimed: 'Never was a better cause lost for want of spirit.' But the last thing that could be said of the Tories was that they were united. They had, too, another fatal flaw. They were not sincere in their Jacobitism. The party of Church and King drank toasts to the Stuarts, but did nothing else to help them. As for the leaders, they were all angling for George's favour, and had he been willing to keep them in their jobs they would have been fervently Hanoverian. As it turned out, Bolingbroke fled to France on 28 March 1715 and openly joined the Pretender, to be followed by the Duke of Ormonde in July. Perhaps they had in mind the cluster of exiled lords in Holland in James II's reign, and remembered how they had come back in triumph. The Earl of Oxford was impeached of high treason by the Commons on 10 June 1715 and committed to the Tower, but after being tried by his peers in 1717 was acquitted. Lansdowne and Windham, with a few other Tory leaders, were imprisoned and that was the end of any pro-Jacobite action so far as England was concerned. Except in the north of England where the Earl of Derwentwater, a young Catholic nobleman, and Thomas Forster, a Protestant and MP for Northumberland, came out in arms for the Pretender on 6 October 1715. The story of this ill-fated affair is recounted below.

Meanwhile, the Pretender himself had not been inactive. First he again sought the aid of the French king but Louis XIV was not called 'Le Grand' for nothing. His experiences during the War of the Spanish Succession had inclined him to take a different view of affairs from when he had told the dying James II that he would look after his son's interests. He declined to assist the Pretender, his excuse being that he was now bound by the Treaty of Utrecht in which he had recognised the Protestant succession.[7]

On this rebuff, the Pretender on 29 August 1714 issued his declaration as James III, setting forth his inalienable right to the crowns of Britain and Ireland and his hope that his people would soon realise the justice of his contention. This action, unaccompanied by anything more positive, achieved nothing.

In the Highlands of Scotland there was known to be unrest among the clans and a movement of some Highlanders towards Inverness. Several noblemen of the Jacobite persuasion were thereupon arrested and the Government issued a proclamation in which £100,000 was offered for the arrest of the Pretender, who was believed to be landing in Scotland on 15 September. He did not arrive until fifteen months later on 22

December 1715, in time to see the ruin of his cause, and when he did come he proved a great disappointment to his followers, showing none of the spirit needed to animate them. It was said openly that it would have been better for him to have sent 5,000 armed men than to have come himself. Had he possessed the gay and martial spirit of his son, Prince Charles Edward, the Young Pretender, he might yet have retrieved the position into which his cause had drifted.

For it was not until 2 August 1715 that the Earl of Mar, leader of the Scottish Jacobites, set out for Scotland to raise the Pretender's standard. The reason for the passage of a year from Queen Anne's death was that, in the interval, 'Bobbing John' (the Earl's nickname) had been trying to ingratiate himself with the new king. Mar had been Secretary of State for Scotland but had been deprived of his office by George I. He made great efforts to convince George of his loyalty, and even persuaded many of the chiefs to sign a loyal address to George, who was referred to therein as 'His Sacred Majesty'. The address was contemptuously rejected by the King.

Having arrived in Scotland, Mar summoned the chiefs to a grand hunting match at Braemar, in Aberdeenshire, this being a pretext for a meeting of Jacobites. The Government also issued a summons to the chiefs, which most disobeyed, to come to Edinburgh. At Braemar, the Earl of Mar set up the Pretender's standard and proclaimed him as James VIII and III. The ball on the top of the standard pole fell off as the standard was being put up, which was regarded as a bad omen by the Highlanders. Mar revealed that he had been appointed by James as his Commander-in-Chief, Scotland, and also declared himself opposed to the Union with England, though he had supported the Treaty of 1707.

The Duke of Argyll was then C-in-C Scotland, but his forces were small, only about 2,000 in all. Mar, on the other hand, was receiving reinforcements amost every day and the 1715 rising was the only time that the majority of the clans took part on the Stuart side. Soon Mar had an army of 10,000–12,000 men with which he took Perth and then, instead of pushing south, waited without any clear motive.[8] Having such a great superiority of numbers, Mar should have been able easily to disperse Argyll's army and march on Edinburgh, instead of which he sent a force under the command of Brigadier Mackintosh of Borlum to aid the English Jacobites. This force was shipped across the Firth of Forth, evaded the English warships in the estuary, and captured Leith. Some time was lost by this exploit which was of no particular value as Mackintosh could not capture Edinburgh owing to the advance of Argyll. At last, on 22 October, Mackintosh set out for Kelso, in Roxburghshire, whither the English Jacobites under Forster were marching. The Lowland Jacobites under the Earl of Kenmure had joined their English brethren on 22 October. Junction with Mackintosh was effected and the whole force amounted to about 2,000 men, of whom 1,400 were foot.

A really useful and important service to the Pretender's cause might have been rendered by this force if the several generals in charge of it could have agreed on a set course of action. The best thing to have done would have been to march to a junction with Mar's men and the Highlanders under General Gordon who were marching to meet them. In this way Argyll would have been taken in rear as well as front and outnumbered eight to one. Instead, great dissension prevailed in the Jacobite councils. The Highlanders refused to march into England but were at length prevailed upon to do so, although 500 of their number thereupon deserted, only to be seized by the Scottish country folk and put in prison. The rest of the army marched to Preston, in Lancashire, under the delusion which was to haunt the Jacobites to the end, that huge numbers of Stuart adherents were waiting to join them. At Preston, the Jacobite army was attacked by General Wills, and later by General Carpenter. Despite a desperate resistance, they were forced to surrender to the number of 1,468 men, 463 of whom were English. No less than 75 of the English were noblemen and gentlemen, and 143 of the Scots, most of these persons of quality being Lowlanders. Unlike the Highland chiefs, the Lowland magnates were unable to bring any large force of vassals with them. This was the last rising in arms of the English Jacobites. The spirit of the Cavaliers was dead.

In Scotland, a very different outlook obtained among the Highlanders. The great danger was that the procrastinating behaviour of 'Bobbing John' might result in the dispersal of his army without a battle. The clansmen were keen to fight.

K

They cared nothing for the monotonous duties of a camp and the fact, well known to all regulars, that 'half a soldier's life is waiting' was meaningless to them. Mar had lost the best campaigning weather in Scotland, the late summer and autumn, and it was not until 10 November that he left Perth and marched to Auchterarder. Argyll had intelligence of this and with an army now nearly 4,000 strong, he crossed Stirling bridge to Dunblane on 12 November. That night the two armies camped (without shelter on the bare ground) about three miles from each other, with only the Sheriffmuir, a waste of moorland, between them.

As soon as Mar became aware of Argyll's nearness he marshalled his men, some 8,000 in number, with a reserve of 400 cavalry. Argyll took longer to form his line of battle and, seeing this, Mar resolved to attack at once and bravely led his men against the half-formed left wing of the enemy. For a moment the Highlanders were checked by the fall of the Captain of Clanranald, Alan Muidartach, who was mortally wounded, but rallied by Glengarry, who shouted: 'Revenge today, mourning tomorrow', the clansmen rushed forward in a fury of ardour. The bayonets of the infantry were dashed aside by the Highlanders' targs and then the broadswords did their work as at Killiecrankie. Argyll's whole left wing gave way. The same fate befell Mar's right wing, though it did not break into such precipitate flight. The Highlanders attacked with the same tactics as elsewhere but this time they were checked by a combination of steady fire and the bayonet. After a protracted contest between the foot, Argyll sent his cavalry to turn their flank and this broke the Jacobite horse and forced their infantry into a damaging retreat.

In this fashion each army could claim to have been victorious. Each of the leaders drew off his men, Mar to Ardoch and Argyll to Dunblane. Indeed, some very amusing verses were written about the battle of Sheriffmuir.[9] One of the Jacobite leaders had observed before the battle that, if there were no action, the Highlanders would retreat; in the event of a battle they would go off with their booty afterwards, and should they be defeated they would go back to their homes. A more resolute commander than Mar might therefore have expected his army to disappear after Sheriffmuir. Strange to recount, some of the clans did little fighting; the Macphersons and Macgregors are said to have taken no part at all in the combat and other satirical verses describe Rob Roy as looking on to see what booty he could catch.[10]

Mar retired to Perth, Argyll to Stirling, but whereas the latter could expect to be reinforced, Mar had to see his army dwindle by the retreat of clan after clan. Inverness was re-captured by Government forces on 13 November, the day on which Borlum and the southern Jacobites were cooped up in Preston. The surrender at Preston and the battle of Sheriffmuir took place on 14 November. Simon Fraser, later Lord Lovat, was instrumental in taking Inverness. Having found that he could not ingratiate himself with the Pretender at St Germains, he became zealous for King George and brought out most of his clan on the Government side.

It was only when the insurrection was petering out that the Pretender arrived at Peterhead, on 22 December 1715. He joined his adherents but his prevailing temper of melancholy had a depressing effect upon them. However, he was proclaimed in various places as King and 23 January had been set for his coronation at Scone. In the meantime Argyll had received reinforcements of good troops from England and Holland and with an army of some 10,000 men he began to advance on Perth.

This news had an invigorating effect upon Mar's soldiers. The prospect of battle delighted them and rallied the clans to the Stuart standard. But when Mar decided to retreat in the face of Argyll's advance and fixed 31 January 1716 as the day—discontent again broke out in his army and 800 of the High-landers marched off into the hills of their own accord.

The Stuart army marched from Perth to Montrose which it reached on 3 February, following a most peculiar route for an army making for the Highlands. It was soon obvious to the rank and file that James VIII and III was getting ready to leave them, and arrangements had to be made for the army to march on to Aberdeen while clandestine plans were operated to disguise James's departure. He was personally brave and aware of how despicable he must appear in deserting those who had risked their lives for him. He was overborne by the advice of his closest friends but he appointed General Gordon as his C-in-C with express powers to treat with the Government. In the course of his stay, James had been responsible for burning the villages of Dunning, Auchterarder, Blackford, Crieff and Muthil in order to add to the difficulties of Argyll's advance in the snows of winter. Before leaving, James wrote to Argyll, telling him that he had left money with some of the local magistrates with which to indemnify the villagers, and asked Argyll to see that the fund was so used."

On 4 February, James embarked on a small French vessel and got safely away after a voyage of five days, landing at Waldam, near Gravelines, in part of Flanders, then under French rule.

The Jacobite army now continued its retreat in orderly fashion through Moray and Strathspey into Badenoch, where it dispersed. Contingents had dropped off on the march as a clan reached its home country. About 160 officers and gentlemen volunteers managed to reach the Orkneys where they boarded two French frigates which carried them to Gothenburg, and the Swedish service.

Everything in the conduct of the 1715 rising was ill-conceived and worse executed. Many hypotheses can be put forward as to the probable consequences if different courses had been followed; if James had come before Sheriffmuir; if Mar had attacked Argyll instead of waiting until the latter was reinforced, and so on. What is certain is that, as a result of the rising, the British Government had seriously to consider the problem of the clans and to take measures, which thirty years later, would complete the ruin of the whole system.

10 The End of Gaeldom

THE NEW KING did not err on the side of weakness. As far as he was concerned, all who had taken part in the rebellion and been apprehended should be put to death as soon as possible. In accordance with the sentiments expressed by Fergus in *Waverley*, the main, if not the only punishment fell upon Englishmen and Lowlanders. Some were tried by court-martial and shot; others who were peers were impeached of high treason in the Commons and brought before the bar of the House of Lords. These peers were Derwentwater, Nithsdale, Wintoun, Nairne and Kenmure. Any appeals to George to show clemency were contemptuously rejected, and on the peers being found guilty of high treason they were condemned to death. Any peers who interceded for them, as did the Earl of Nottingham, who was Lord President of the Council, were at once dismissed from office by the King. On the night before his execution the Earl of Nithsdale, dressed in woman's clothes, escaped with the help of his wife. Derwentwater and Kenmure were beheaded on Tower Hill. The Earl of Wintoun escaped to France, and Lord Nairne's life was spared. The other Jacobite prisoners, including Mr Forster and Brigadier Mackintosh of Borlum, were all tried and quickly found guilty of treason which, of course, they were from the Government's point of view. Mackintosh and Forster both got away to the Continent, along with several others, and the ease with which the escapes were made from Newgate, and more especially from the Tower, suggests connivance on the part of the warders or heavy bribery, or both. Having held his Queen captive for very many years—in fact she never came to England—George I must have wondered at the ease with which State prisoners in England made their getaway.

George showed little gratitude to those who had helped his cause and the Duke of Argyll, whose skill had put down the rising in Scotland, was forthwith dismissed from his posts. In his place, George appointed General Carpenter as C-in-C in Scotland. The Duke of Argyll's brother, the Earl of Islay, was dismissed from his post as Lord Registrar of Scotland and the Duke of Montrose appointed in his stead.

Forfeiture of the Scottish leaders did not lag behind, but in Scotland it was not so easy to punish a family by attainting the head. Arrangements were common by which, in the event of a rising, one son went to the rebels while another son, or the father, stayed at home to look after the estate. It was quite common for close kinsmen to be on opposite sides, thus providing insurance against total ruin. In some cases the person appointed to manage a forfeited estate was either a friend or agent of the former owner, and after the '15 many exiled owners had their rents remitted to them by such loyal helpers.

Still something had to be done to pacify the Highlanders and to prevent them from rising in such numbers. General Cadogan had followed up the bands of clansmen who were still at loose in the remote Highlands, and had encountered hardly any resistance. Some chiefs, like Sir Donald MacDonald of Skye, thought it best to escape to France, and from that country now came three ships carrying military supplies—typical of French support for the Stuarts in that it was always either too little or too late. One of these vessels was captured by the Royal Navy; the others got back to France with some seventy Jacobite gentlemen.

The execution of so many Jacobites had caused a revulsion of feeling in England and in 1717 the King was persuaded to grant a free and general pardon to all persons who had before 6 May 1717 committed any treasonable offences. Excepted from the amnesty were the Macgregors and anyone guilty of treason who had gone overseas and then returned without the King's permission.

Meanwhile, in 1716, James had been forced to leave France and live in Rome. As Britain and France were at peace, the British Government could reasonably request the removal from French territory of a person who claimed the British throne. James had to seek helpers elsewhere among the powers of

Europe, and for a time Charles XII of Sweden appeared to offer the best means of assistance. It was always the same story; when a foreign power had a difference with England it was willing to contemplate giving help to the Pretender, but when that disagreement was composed he obtained no further assistance. In 1717 Spain and the Holy Roman Empire were at war, and England, under the Treaty of Utrecht, was in defensive alliance with the Emperor. It was, therefore, possible for the Spanish Prime Minister, Alberoni, later a Cardinal, to take James's side and to despatch a fleet carrying 5,000 men and arms for 30,000 against Britain in 1719. The enterprise miscarried completely, for the Spanish fleet was wrecked in a storm. Two ships, with 300 Spanish troops and some Jacobite leaders, got to Scotland and advanced up Glenshiel with some clansmen in support. They were soon rounded up by the Government troops; the clansmen, mostly Macgregors and Mackenzies, melted away and the Spaniards surrendered as prisoners-of-war. The leaders got away to fight another day, among them Lord George Murray, the Prince's general in the '45.

Simon Fraser, now Lord Lovat, was at that stage in his devious career when he was high in favour with George I. Over the next thirty years he was to intrigue and counter-plot with both Stuart and Hanoverian but, for the present, he was wholeheartedly Hanoverian and drew up a memorial on the Highlanders for the King. He had the best sources of information and when he wrote that the worst evil in the mountains was the continued depredations and robberies, and the general lawlessness, he wrote of what he knew at first-hand. He was perfectly correct in adding that the method of fire and sword had proved useless and that it was impossible to catch the cattle-lifters by the ordinary methods of apprehension of thieves. Two methods of dealing with the theft of cattle were known. One was the payment of blackmail (from 'black' and 'mal'—tribute) by cattle owners, particularly in those parts of the Lowlands adjacent to the Highlands. If the payments were regularly made, the chief in the area in question saw to it that the Lowlanders' cattle were not lifted by any of his clan or by other persons under his control. Like the American gangsters, a chief had his own area which he jealously preserved, and in the event of an interloper breaking into his territory and committing thefts, he would usually undertake to recapture the stolen property or make it up to the person who had paid protection money to him.

This system could obviously make only for lawlessness. Many of the best chiefs refused to tolerate it and no one was more determined to stamp it out among his own people than Cameron of Lochiel.

Lovat's memorial referred to the second and better method, the institution of the Independent Companies. These were composed of men of the same race as the thieves, clansmen who knew the country and how to track down a marauding band. The companies, instituted under William III, had done much to check the robberies. On their disbandment in 1717 these soon began again. As the companies were the origin of one of the most famous Highland regiments, their story may be taken out of its chronological sequence.

In fact, the first companies were originally raised in 1667 for a form of military police duty, as described above. The idea of reforming them came up again in 1739 when six companies were raised. The name 'Independent' was given to them because each of the six was distinct and independent of the others. Three of them were called large companies as each consisted of 100 men, the other three, the smaller companies as they were named, were of 75 men each. The large companies were captained by Lord Lovat, Sir Duncan Campbell of Lochnell and Colonel Grant of Ballindallock; the other three were commanded by Colonel Alexander Campbell of Finab, John Campbell of Carrick, and George Munro of Culcairn. They were a fine body of men with a high proportion of gentlemen serving in the ranks as privates. At a time when the Disarming Act was depriving the Highlanders of their weapons, the officers and men of the Independent Companies were able to bear arms. Their duties were to keep down the disaffected and to prevent robberies, and to this end they were stationed in small detachments in various parts of the country. They were called the Black Watch because they were to deal principally with the instances of blackmail. As near as possible, they wore the same tartan and claim that their name derived from its sombre hues of black, green and blue. In 1739 it was decided to form four additional companies comprising 1,000 men and to make the whole into a regiment of the line. The Earl of Crawford was appointed to command the regiment, which was raised in 1740 in Perthshire and known as the 43rd Foot. In 1749 it became the 42nd. The tartan used became standardised under mass-production as the Black Watch tartan. It was also known as the Campbell tartan, because three of the original six companies were commanded by Campbells. It was further claimed by Grants and Munros as their clan tartan on similar grounds. The tartans of later Highland regiments are based on that of the Black Watch.

In 1743 the newly raised regiment was sent to Flanders. At first, many of the soldiers objected to leaving Scotland and going abroad. Some mutinied and even attempted to march back to Scotland, but were persuaded to rejoin and duly fought in Flanders. When British troops were recalled because of the '45 rebellion, the 43rd (as they then were) were among those recalled and were stationed in Kent. Three other companies which had been raised were kept in Scotland during the rebellion. One of them served at Prestonpans and the others were in the Highlands. After Culloden they acted with the rest of Cumberland's army in devastating the country of the rebels.

Returning from this digression, the next great step in dealing with the Highlands was the Disarming Act, by which the clans were required to give up their weapons. This and the next move—the building of proper roads where previously there had been tracks only, if tracks there were—came under the supervision of General, later Field Marshal, George Wade. His name is always treated with respect by Highland writers and he is usually described as a gentleman. It is to be feared that this term was generously applied to him mainly because he refrained from pressing his inquiries about concealed arms too far, as well as because of his fair and honourable treatment of the chiefs.

The Government were not entirely satisfied with the bona fides of Lord Lovat's report but took it seriously enough to appoint Wade to a commission in order to examine and recommend on the state of the Highlands. This was in July 1724 and Wade's report agreed substantially with Lovat's. He stated that there were about 22,000 men in the Highlands capable of bearing arms, and that these were divided roughly into equal parts, owning allegiance to Government and to the Stuarts. Forbes of Culloden, in his breakdown of the numbers of potential combatants made some twenty-three years later, gives the numbers for each clan, reaching a total of 32,000. This is more likely to be accurate but the rest of Wade's estimate as to character and conduct is probably correct. Whatever the facts, Wade had the primary task of disarming the clans. He was a professional soldier who had served in the army from the age of seventeen and seen much of continental warfare. Like many others of his profession, he found the Highlanders a serious problem, and though he succeeded in disarming the Whig or Government clans, he failed with the Jacobites.

The Disarming Act allowed for compensation to be paid for surrendered arms. Naturally, worthless worn-out arms were handed in, and to make up sufficient numbers, other old and useless weapons were secured from abroad, up to £13,000 worth. In his report made in January 1725-6, Wade wrote that the Earl of Seaforth's clan had been disarmed. Apparently this was genuine, as the Mackenzies were no longer of service to the Stuarts. At Brahan Castle, several clans mustered to lay down their swords and muskets, among them the Macdonalds of Glengarry, Clanranald and Glencoe, the Camerons and the Appin Stuarts, and the clans of Atholl and of Breadalbane. The total of weapons surrendered came to 2,685, yet 6,000 muskets were brought over in 1719 and were not accounted for. Perhaps a more ruthless and less gentlemanly commander would have insisted on a drastic search of the glens in overwhelming force. As it was, the Whig clans, who had no sources abroad from which they could obtain new weapons, became relatively defenceless—which accounts for their failure to act on the Government side in the '45—whereas the Jacobite clans were able to conceal many of their arms. Thus the Disarming Act did not succeed in bringing peace to the Highlands, though the incidence of robbery was greatly reduced owing to the presence of the Independent Companies and the efforts made by the chiefs. Broken clans like the Macgregors still continued to steal, but this was mainly because they had no other means of livelihood.

General Wade proceeded to make roads into the Highlands, the first that were ever constructed there. Some writers regard these roadways as the preliminary to the infamous Highland clearances; in truth, the roads were laid out as one would expect of a professional soldier. There is an old jingle oft quoted about them:

'Had you seen these roads before they were made,
You would lift up your hands and bless General Wade.'

The natives did not like the hard gravel of the roads. Accustomed to travelling barefoot over their heaths and hills, they found the new roads very hard and painful, even with their thin brogues. Wade also superintended the building of forty stone bridges and the chiefs feared that by using them to cross the streams instead of wading, the clansmen would become weakened and degenerate.

Wade's roads were strategically planned. The main highway began at Perth and passed through Dunkeld and Blair Atholl to Dalnacardock in Perthshire. There it was joined by a road starting from Stirling by Crieff, going through Glenalmond to Aberfeldy, where it crossed the Tay by one of Wade's more famous bridges. From Dalnacardock, it branched in two directions, one road going through Garva Moor and over the Corryarrick mountain (which divides Glenmore and Upper Strathspey) to Fort Augustus. The other branch went north to Ruthven in Badenoch, and via Delmagery to Inverness. Yet another of Wade's roads joined Forts Augustus and William by a route beside Loch Ness and Loch Lochy. Wade's further proposals were for the strengthening of the forts, the building of barracks at Inverness, the stationing of cavalry between Perth and Inverness, and the placing of a naval vessel in Loch Ness.

James, in the meantime, had decided to perpetuate his dynasty, and on 28 May 1719 he married the Princess Clementina, daughter of Prince James Lewis Sobieski, son of John, King of Poland. On 31 December 1720, Prince Charles Edward (Bonnie Prince Charlie) was born, and on 21 March 1725, Henry Benedict, who became a priest and later Cardinal York. With these two the male line of Stuart ended but not before the elder boy had shown one last gleam of Stuart romance and brilliancy. The Stuart family, by now very short of money, resided in Italy, often in Rome under the protection of the Pope.

During the period between Wade's work in the Highlands

and the outbreak of the '45, the clans were supposed to have been quiet. Two true stories can help us to understand what their previous state may have been, if for these twenty years they were reckoned quiet. A Lord of Session, Lord Grange, suffered much domestic discord with his wife. He was of the Jacobite persuasion and Lady Grange took some imprudent letters of his to the Lord Justice Clerk. She went to Edinburgh on her way to London and Grange, in terror lest Jacobite names should come out, had her abducted to St Kilda, a most lonely island. There she remained for two years, until she was removed to Skye, where she died in 1745. In the other story, the Laird of Glengarry, deciding to get rid of his wife, had her taken to a barren rock in the sea, where she died. This was in 1727.

In England there was discontent with the Government because of the King's deep interest in his Hanoverian dominions, a not unnatural feeling on his part since he had been born there. So, too, had his son, George II, who succeeded him in 1727 and was more popular than his father. There was a tradition in the royal house of Hanover of hostility between the reigning sovereign and his eldest son,[1] and this unfortunate state of affairs lasted right up until the accession of Edward VII to the throne; between him and his heir, the future George V, a cordial relationship existed. Between George I and his son there was a particularly bitter hatred, as there was also between George II and his heir, the Prince of Wales, the father of George III. The existence of such a family hatred encouraged the growth of a Prince's party, people who looked to the new monarch for favours which they could not obtain from the old. George II, therefore, had a following when he came to the throne which his father had lacked. He was personally brave and showed well at Dettingen in 1743, the last battle in which a British sovereign took part.

Each year that the Hanoverians reigned made their displacement more unlikely. Discontent in England with the Government, and even with the sovereign, did not mean that the discontented wanted to change the dynasty. Exiles grow out of touch with the country they have left, and from many examples in the twentieth century of emigré governments without hope of restoration it is possible to gauge the extent of Jacobite support in Britain. James sent over agents to discover the feelings of his subjects towards him. The French Government also from time to time sought reports as to the sort of support which might be expected from English Jacobites. In the summer of 1743 a Mr Butler, who was an equerry to Louis XV, came to England under the pretence of purchasing horses, but in reality to gain intelligence as to the Jacobite feeling in England. It is impossible to better Lang's account of the completely erroneous information given to Butler. 'He was introduced to Colonel Cecil and to the English leaders. He was given to believe that in the Common Council and aldermen, 196 out of 236 were Jacobites. He was taken to the country houses of the nobles, and to Lichfield races, where all the gentry, 300 in number, prayed for a Restoration, and he received a list of seventy Jacobite peers. The list is printed and is extremely imposing.' (*History*, vol 4, p 438.) A faith inspired by such enthusiasm for James could be expected to topple George II from his throne, or at least to justify French help, and one would like to know how French military intelligence evaluated Mr Butler's findings. It is hard to believe that as good a soldier as Marshal Saxe did not wonder why the English Jacobites, if they had such a strong feeling for the Stuarts, had made so feeble a showing in the '15.

However, by that time, 1743, France was once more in conflict with England, in the War of the Austrian Succession, though no declaration was made until March 1744! A diversion which would seriously damage the British war effort and necessitate the recall of British troops would be very much in France's favour, and the one planned was to be on a massive scale. There were to be 15,000 troops under the command of no less than Marshal Saxe, and the transports were to be escorted by thirteen ships of the line. The armada assembled at Boulogne, Calais and Dunkirk with the object of effecting a landing in Kent. At the same time as the Kent invasion, a smaller force was to be landed in Scotland under the command of the Earl Marischal. There the Government forces consisted of one regiment of dragoons, three regiments of foot, and the Independent Companies, though the last were soon to be formed into the Black Watch and leave Scotland.

James himself did not feel like accompanying the expedition, but suggested his elder son, Charles, now twenty-three years old, known to be as enthusiastic as his father was gloomy, ardent, high-spirited and quite unruly. Under cover of participating in a boar hunt, Charles and his brother Henry left Rome. Henry went to Cisterna, but Charles journeyed on to Paris where he had interviews with Saxe and with Louis XV. Intelligence of his arrival in France at last reached the British Government, and the juxtaposition of a French fleet in the Channel with Prince Charles's presence at Dunkirk at once alerted the Government to the real object of the French preparations. The position was serious. The Government had only 16,000 regular troops in the country. (According to another account, and one more likely to be accurate, only 6,000.) The main force of the Royal Navy, the strongest barrier to invasion, was absent in the Mediterranean. However, by extraordinary efforts, the Government collected a powerful fleet under Sir John Norris, and at the same time made strenuous efforts to put the south coast defences in order. Under a treaty with Holland, the British Government was able to demand 6,000 Dutch troops in case of need. These were promptly granted and duly arrived to help in saving England from 'a Popish pretender', the term used in the addresses of both Lords and Commons to the King. Messages of loyalty to the Crown and pledges of support poured in, and promptly showed the falsity of Jacobite hopes.

Sir John Norris gathered his fleet and sailed into the Downs in search of the French vessels, which he found still at anchor, with only half the troops yet embarked in the transports. If Saxe could have been allowed the six hours' freedom of the Channel for which Napoleon sought, he could have got his men to England. Norris anchored two leagues from the French, intending to attack them next morning but the French admiral, not liking the prospect, weighed anchor after sunset and succeeded in getting down Channel to Brest. Then a violent storm, almost a hurricane, arose, but the elements which forced the British warships to slip their cables and be driven before the wind, also wrought vast damage in Saxe's transports. Saxe had been accompanied by the Prince, whose hopes must have been at their highest as he saw the French soldiers going aboard, but after the storm all was over as far as any further substantial French aid for the Jacobite cause was concerned.

For some months Prince Charles lived in France in a well-pierced incognito. The British and French were now formally and actually at war, and on 11 May 1745 the French won the battle of Fontenoy, where great losses were sustained by the British. Charles judged the time ripe for his next adventure. Two vessels, the *Elizabeth* and the *Doutelle*, were placed at his disposal by two West Indian merchants, Ruttledge and Walsh, and on 5 July he sailed from Belleisle on board the *Doutelle* accompanied by the Seven Men of Moidart or more. On the subject of the numbers, discrepancies occur in the various accounts. The total of seven can be reached by excluding (1) Buchanan employed as a messenger to Rome by Cardinal Tencin; (2) Duncan Cameron, formerly a servant at Boulogne of the older Lochiel, and (3) Anthony Walsh, owner of the *Doutelle*, also some persons of 'inferior condition'. The *Elizabeth* carried 2,000 muskets and 500 French broadswords.

On 9 July, a British warship, the *Lion* of 60 guns commanded by Captain Brett, was sighted west of the Lizard. A fierce fight between the *Lion* and the *Elizabeth* ensued and after five hours both vessels were little more than wrecks. The *Elizabeth* went back to France while the *Doutelle*, which had taken no part in the fight, went on to Scotland. On 11 July a vessel was sighted which gave chase but the *Doutelle* out-sailed her. On sighting land (part of the Hebrides) an English man-of-war was seen, whereupon Walsh altered course and made his landfall at Eriskay, the largest of a cluster of rocky islands lying off South Uist. There the Prince landed on 23 July having been eighteen days at sea.

The strangest discrepancies exist as to the dates of the Prince's journey, and those given above are from Keltie, op cit, vol 2, pp 512–13. Andrew Lang, *History*, vol 4, p 458 gives 13 July as the date when the *Doutelle* joined the *Elizabeth*. They set sail for Scotland on 15 July. On 20 July the battle with the *Lion* took place. The *Doutelle* sighted Bernera on 22 July to 2 August and on the following day Charles landed on Eriskay. For Charles's voyage to Lochnanuagh in Arisaig and his landing at Borradale. Lang gives the dates 25 July to 5 August. Frank Adams in his (1908) *Clans, Septs, etc*, simply says that the Prince landed at Moidart (on the coast of Inverness-shire) in July. Sir Thomas Innes in his edition of Adam's work (1960) said (p 65) that the Prince sailed from France on 21 June, and landed on Eriskay on 23 July. 'Next day the ship sailed on to Loch-man-uamh in Arisaig and the Prince landed. On 11 August he went to Kinlochmoidart'. *The Encyclopedia Britannica*, under 'Charles Edward', gives 13 July as the date of sailing from Nantes, 20 July as the day of battle with the *Lion*, and 3 August for the landing on Eriskay. The authors of *Battles of the '45* (Katherine Tomasson and Francis Buist, 1962 and 1967, p 24) nearly agree with Keltie, giving 4 July for the sailing of the *Dowtelle* from Belle Isle, the landing on Eriskay being on 23 July. *Chambers' Encyclopedia*, under 'Jacobites', gives no dates for voyage or landing, beyond 1745, and *Haydn's Dictionary of Dates* (1873) says, under 'Pretenders', that Prince Charles landed in Scotland and proclaimed his father king on 25 July 1745.

These discrepancies in dates in the several modern accounts are strange, but all the narratives agree on two points, the cold reception that the Prince received and yet the fact that he set up the Stuart standard on 19 August 1745 in Glenfinnan in south-west Inverness-shire. On his arrival, dressed in the garb of a minister, the Prince sent for MacDonald of Boisdale, Clanranald's brother, in South Uist, whose advice was an uncomprising 'Go home'. To this the Prince replied 'I am home'. Messages were sent to MacDonald of Sleat and to Macleod. Neither would join the Prince, and Macleod at once, on 3 August, sent information and warnings about Charles to Forbes of Culloden. The Prince continued his efforts to win over the chiefs, all of whom advised him of the desperate nature of the enterprise and that it would be better for him to return to France. The fact that he did gain the support of these generous hearts is abundant proof of the gay gallantry and wonderful charm which marked this Prince of romance at the time. No help from France could explain it, for even the weapons on the *Elizabeth* had been lost; there was nothing but the heir of the Stuarts summing up in his person the last brilliant glories of his race. How, then, did he win the chiefs to follow him? 'Will you not aid me?' were his words to Ranald MacDonald, the young brother of Kinlochmoidart. 'I will, though no other man in the Highlands should draw his sword.' To Cameron of Lochiel's (the gentle Lochiel's) caution,

Charles found the right reply, 'Then Lochiel can read in the newspapers the fate of his Prince.'

The secret of Charles's presence was out, and on 1 August the British Government set a price of £30,000 on his head, a sum so great as to be almost, if not completely, inconceivable to a Highlander. The setting of the price was a direct incitement to murder, yet even when the Prince's shooting star, after its brief passage across the heavens, sank into darkness, there was none who yielded to this temptation to gain untold wealth.

The sentiments which actuated the Prince were those of the gallant Montrose. He sent away the *Doutelle*, so there could be no retreat. On 16 August some of Keppoch's and Glengarry's men ambushed and captured two companies of the Royal Scots between Spean bridge and Loch Lochy. Sir John Cope, commander of the Government forces in Scotland, could ill spare any soldiers for he had only about 3,000 men in the country, and they were scattered in detachments. Cope began to concentrate his men at Stirling by 8 August. Now the results of the Disarming Act were felt. 'Argyll, without orders from the Government, could not arm the Campbells, and the Whig clans had obeyed the orders for disarmament.' (Lang, op cit, vol 4, p 460.) Disarmed, the Whig clans could do nothing during the insurrection; but the Jacobite clans could unearth their weapons.

Cope has been subjected to much ridicule (the famous song, 'Hey Johnnie Cope are ye walking yet', will never be forgotten), but he had in fact a better appreciation of the situation than anyone else in power in Scotland. He asked for artillery, and especially for artillerymen, for though there were cannons and mortars in Edinburgh Castle there was not a single royal artilleryman under Cope's command. Considering the terrible havoc wrought by Cumberland's artillery at Culloden, he was obviously right in his urgent request for the artillery arm. Cope was an experienced soldier who had served in Spain and at Dettingen and by 1739 had reached the rank of major-general.

The troops now under his command, however, were not such as to inspire him with much confidence. His cavalry consisted of two dragoon regiments, Gardiner's and Hamilton's, recruited

L

mainly in Ireland. Having seen no service, the men were ill-disciplined and their horses not properly trained or used to gunfire. As for the infantry, they were the regiments of Murray (57th) and Lascelles (58th), and a half regiment of Lee (55th), none of which had ever been in action and indeed had only been raised in 1741. In addition there was Guise's regiment (6th), which was raised in 1674 and had something of a regimental tradition. Most of the Independent Companies were, as previously mentioned, formed into the Black Watch and either stationed in the south of Scotland or overseas. There were garrisons in the castles of Edinburgh, Stirling and Dumbarton and also in Fort Augustus and Fort William and these held out. Even when the Prince's army captured Edinburgh, the Castle remained in Government hands and its artillery fired on the Jacobites as they marched towards England. Fort Augustus was captured after the Prince's forces had retreated to the Highlands.

The movements of the two armies were complicated by the double-dealing of men who afterwards came out for the Prince. Lord George Murray, a younger son of the Duke of Atholl, met Cope on 21 August and made light of the rising. Later he joined the Prince and became his general, but there was never any cordiality between them and towards the end, open hostility. Lord Lovat was playing his usual double game of siding simultaneously with Government and with Prince. Eventually he sent out his son, Simon, to lead his clan, the Frasers.

At Glenfinnan, where a monument to him was erected in 1815, Prince Charles had about 1,500 to 2,000 men. Most of them were Macdonalds, with the Stuarts of Appin and 700 Camerons brought by Lochiel. Cope marched northward to Inverness which he reached on 29 August, while the Highland army was posted near the Corryarrach Pass. If the hesitant clans, particularly the Frasers, had joined earlier Cope's army might have been surrounded and destroyed, and it is just possible that the Whig clans might then have joined the Jacobites. However, Charles led his army through the Highlands to Dunkeld. On 4 September Cope marched from Inverness to Aberdeen, where he put his men on board ship and on 12 September sailed for Leith. The Prince's army marched on, past Stirling, while the regiments of dragoons simply retreated before them. Crossing the Forth unopposed, the Highlanders succeeded in entering Edinburgh on 16 September. They had spent a week in Perth where they were joined by the Duke of Perth and Lord George Murray, the latter being appointed by the Prince as his lieutenant-general. The Macgregors were out once more for the royal house which had shown them favour, so were the Robertsons of Struan, the Menzies and the Maclachlans. In Edinburgh, James VIII and III was proclaimed at the Mercat Cross and Charles held court at Holyrood in the palace of his ancestors.

Cope's ill-assorted and ill-prepared army of not more than 3,000 men reached Dunbar and took up position at Prestonpans, some 9½ miles east of Edinburgh. There, on 21 September, the two armies met in a conflict which was over in ten minutes. Cope had obtained some artillery but barely more than two or three experienced men to man the pieces. Even so, the limited fire-power of five 1½ pounder guns and six mortars badly shook the clansmen who, having dropped their plaids, were advancing at great speed with a hideous roar. At the discharge of the guns the redcoats cheered; but the Highlanders quickly recovered and, with an answering shout, came on. The royal troops began to waver; the dragoons refused to charge into the clans and the artillery guard cowered behind the guns. The cavalry fled and the infantry were left to meet the full force of wave after wave of clansmen. Cope rode into the infantry to try to rally them but without avail, and the whole line broke and fled. About 300–500 men were killed, about the same number wounded, and some 1,600 captured. Cope, with some of the dragoons, carried the news of his defeat to Berwick.

Except for the isolated garrisons, the royal forces in Scotland had disintegrated. Prince Charles had control of Scotland to the extent that his forces could range at will, taking what they pleased and paying off old scores. Frasers, Ogilvies from Angus, Gordons of Glenbucket, Mackinnons of Machim, and Macphersons of Cluny joined the Highland army. The Prince had a small but well-mounted and organised body of cavalry, Lowlanders for the most part, but there was no real accession of ardent Jacobites from the Lowlands. Above all, the northern clans—Mackays, Sutherlands and Munros—and the Macleans, with large sections of the Mackenzies, Mackintoshes, Gordons and Grants, were for the Government. The Mackintosh chief held a commission in the Black Watch and remained on the Government side, but his wife, 'Colonel Anne', raised a regiment from the clan for the Prince.

After the great success of Prestonpans the Jacobite leaders had to decide upon their next course of action. The situation in England was that the Government had organised three armies formed of regular troops. The 6,000 Dutch soldiers could not be used owing to the Treaty of Tournay between France and Holland, by which the Dutch were barred from fighting against France and an ally of hers. To make the latter stipulation operative, a sham treaty of alliance (it was nothing else) was concluded between Louis XV and James, the Old Pretender. The British Government called back from Flanders three battalions of the Guards, eighteen regiments of the line, nine squadrons of cavalry and four companies of artillery, which greatly reinforced the small body of regular troops in the country. Thus three armies were formed. One, under Field Marshal Wade who had been recalled to active service at the age of seventy-two, was marching towards Newcastle. The second army, at first under Lieutenant-General Sir John Ligonier, and later under Cumberland's command, was meant for the north-west of England. The third army was stationed on the south-east coast to meet a possible French invasion but as the threat of this receded with the Royal Navy's command of the narrow seas, it was moved to London to guard the capital. In all, some 30,000 regular troops were getting ready to deal with the rising.

Charles was sanguine as to the imminence of a French landing and of a rising in force of English Jacobites once he entered England. He favoured the direct approach, an advance to Newcastle to seek battle with Wade. His advisers were against leaving Scotland, but as Charles was determined on entering England they at last agreed to a plan proposed by Lord George Murray. By this it was agreed to march through the Border country and enter England by way of Cumberland. On 3 November 1745 the Prince's army of 5,000 foot and 500 cavalry left Edinburgh and on 9 November approached Carlisle. The city was very weakly defended and surrendered.

Wade's army moved very slowly through deep snow and reached Hexham on 18 November, in time to learn of Carlisle's capitulation. Wade then took his army back to Newcastle.

Leaving 100 men to garrison Carlisle Castle, the Prince began his southern march on 20–21 November. Inevitably he had lost some of the clansmen by desertion, and his invading army did not number more than 5,000. On 26 November Charles reached Preston, where a member of an old Catholic family, Francis Townley, with two of the Vaughans and a Mr Morgan from Wales, joined the Pretender's colours. At every town the Jacobites proclaimed James VIII and III but no man bade them Godspeed. In Manchester alone, reached on 29–30 November, was there any enthusiasm, and here some 200 men joined Charles, and were placed under the command of Townley as the Manchester Regiment. Beyond this there was not a flicker from the English Jacobites. Lord George succeeded in out-manoeuvring Cumberland, who was now in command in the Midlands, and the Jacobites entered Derby on 4 December. After a stormy meeting on 5 December, the Prince was forced to agree to his council-of-war's decision to retreat and this began on 6 December. With no care for his own safety, the Prince wanted desperately to march on towards London, confident in the invincibility of his clansmen, and the belief that some of the Government troops would desert to his side.

It is always easy to be wise after the event and to be brave vicariously. Had the Prince's army marched on—5,000 men against the 30,000 of the Government's three armies combined —they must surely have succumbed to sheer numbers and the destructive power of skilful musketry and devastating artillery fire. Yet had the last Jacobite army gone down to a crushing defeat in the heart of England, with the Prince killed in battle, the consequent legend would have been heroic. So, in fact, it was at Culloden, and had the Prince died then in the battle, nothing would have marred his fame. The idea of the whole adventure was the Prince's own. His father had certainly not encouraged it; and if the Prince had had genuine expectations of French help, he had yet sailed to Scotland without it. Once in Scotland, he had been advised by his most loyal adherents to return to France, but by his gallant personality and address he had persuaded them to join him against their better judgement.

By his action, the Prince had put in total jeopardy the lives, the property and the families of his adherents, but he had shown that he had no regard for his own life. The fourteen months during which he was in Britain were to be called very truly by the Highlanders the 'Prince's Year'. To that period of bright personal achievement his life had been directed; when it was over and he was safe once more on the Continent, he had only the memory of that high adventure, and the dying hope that it could be renewed, to sustain him in the forty-two years in which this once gay and gallant adventurer sank through drink to his death in 1788.

With the decision to retreat, the stage in this narrative is reached, at which, to use a colloquialism, 'we came in'. Certain features of the Highlanders' march should, however, be mentioned. They paid for any supplies on the march to Derby and were remarkable for their outstandingly good behaviour; yet instead of commentators and observers recognising its merit, it was merely noted as astonishing conduct on the part of savages and banditti. So well had the Lowland hatred of the Gael been transmitted to the English that it was commonly believed in England that the Highlanders were cannibals. When Lochiel, the gentle Lochiel, entered an English peasant's hut to pay for some goods, the poor woman begged him to spare her children.

In the retreat, the Government army at last caught up with the Jacobites at Clifton Moor, in Westmorland. There was a skirmish between the Prince's rearguard and some of Cumberland's dragoons—the last armed conflict on English soil, as Sedgemoor was the last battle. In this skirmish there were about 70–80 casualties, including a dozen killed on either side. The dragoons had been issued with iron skull-caps, on which several of the Highlanders broke their broadswords. There was no further attempt at pursuit, so that Charles was able to claim Clifton as another little victory. The snow and the icy roads made the pace of a regular army much slower than that of the nimble Highlanders. At Carlisle, the Prince abandoned his artillery and also abandoned, for that was what it was, some 400 men under John Hamilton, who was the factor of the Duke of Gordon. This was on 19 December and by 30 December the Duke of Cumberland had reduced Carlisle and forced the garrison to surrender. On 20 December the Highlanders forded the Esk into Scotland, exhibiting the greatest joy at being over the Border. Lord Strathallan, who was at Perth collecting forces for the Prince, wrote encouraging letters and there were the usual delusive promises from the French about grand forces about to arrive. Some small French succours had actually landed but not in any sufficient number to turn the scale. The broken reed of the French assistance was something on which the Prince leaned to the end.

Charles returned to a Scotland where Government forces were mustering strongly. Edinburgh was occupied by General Hawley, who had succeeded Cope. Lord Loudoun held Inverness for the Government with some Independent Companies and his own regiment. Major-General John Campbell was drilling the Campbell militia.

Strathallan had about 4,000 men, of whom about 750 were French and Irish soldiers (the French succours); the rest were latecomers from the clans, Frasers, Mackintoshes, Farquharsons. Had the Prince been able to keep this force, plus that which had retreated from Derby under his banner, he might yet have had some hope of victory, at least in Scotland.

The Lowlands of Scotland were solid against the Prince; English Jacobites had shown conclusively what their support was worth; the British fleet guarded the whole island and was able to stop any major attempt at invasion. Cumberland was recalled to the south, however, to meet the invasion threat and Hawley was entrusted with the task of beating Charles.

The Prince had marched to Perth to join Lord Strathallan, who now possessed some artillery sent from France and with this the Jacobites began the siege of Stirling Castle. Hawley marched to meet the Prince's forces and the battle took place at Falkirk on 17 January 1746. In an area of confining slopes and ravines a battle unsatisfactory to both sides was fought. Hawley succeeded in withdrawing his force with the loss of his guns and his camp, and about 400 dead; while the Highlanders are reputed to have lost about forty killed, some estimates give fifty. Once again both infantry and cavalry fled before the Highland charge. In Hawley's orders dated 12 January there is an accurate account of the Highland method of fighting and how to deal with it, and had his troops been properly trained in this they might have ended the rebellion at Falkirk. As it was, several of the regiments which broke there regained their morale and were successful at Culloden.

After the victory at Falkirk there was little jubilation in the Jacobite army, but rather despondency. Hawley's right wing had stood firm, poured in a heavy fire on the Highlanders' flank and then retreated in good order. It was not a helpful augury, for here were regular troops unshaken by the clansmen.

To crush the rebels, the Government chose the only man capable in their opinion of the feat. The Duke of Cumberland, younger son of George II, arrived in Edinburgh on 30 January to assume command. He was four months younger than Charles, a professional soldier who had commanded at Fontenoy. It is often forgotten that Stuart and Hanoverian kings and princes were of the same stock. Prince Charles and Cumberland were cousins, both Stuart and Hanoverian having gained the throne of Scotland and England through the female line.

With reinforcements of foot and horse and a train of artillery under regular army gunners, the Duke advanced on 31 January to Linlithgow. On 1 February the Jacobite army began its retreat from Stirling northward. Lord George Murray and the chiefs held the view that during the winter they would capture the Forts William and Augustus and gather 10,000 men for battle in the spring. Prince Charles was very much opposed to the policy of retreat and was probably right in his opinion that it would lower morale. By 20 February the Highland army was at Inverness. Fort Augustus was captured after a week's siege and some of the Government troops were driven out of the area. The Campbell garrisons were raided and surrendered.

The Prince had lost interest in military matters after his views had been rejected. Cumberland advanced steadily, making no attempt at pursuit but taking care to train his men in the way to deal with the Highlanders. The advice previously referred to —in Hawley's Order Book of 12 January 1746—was evidently repeated in Cumberland's orders and certainly formed the basis of the training given to the Government troops.[2] It is as follows:

> The manner of the Highlanders' way of fighting, which there is nothing so easy to resist if officers and men are not possessed of the lies and accounts which are told of them. They commonly form their front rank of what they call their best men or true Highlanders, the number of which being always but few. When they form in battalions, they

commonly form four deep, and these Highlanders form the front of the four and the rest being Lowlanders and arrant scum. When these battalions come within a large musket shot or three score yards, this front gives their fire and immediately throw down their firelocks and come down in a cluster with their swords and targets, making a noise and endeavouring to pierce the body or battalion before them— becoming 12 or 14 deep by the time they come up to the people they attack. The sure way to demolish them is, at three deep, to fire by ranks diagonally to the centre, where they come, the rear rank not to fire till they are within ten or twelve paces; but if the fire is given at a distance, you probably will be broke, for you never get time to load a second cartridge and if you give way, you may give your foot for dead, for they being without a firelock or any load, no man with his arms, accoutrements etc., can escape them, and they give no quarter; but if you will but observe the above directions they are the most despicable enemy that are.

There are two minor inaccuracies in the above. The Highland ranks were not filled up with Lowlanders and they did take prisoners. The 'no quarter' statement was responsible for some frightful actions by British troops after Culloden. In the most important respect, however, the order is completely accurate and, as will be seen, had a far-reaching effect on the training and tactics of British infantry. Another special drill was evolved in the training of the infantry in order to counter the Highlanders' use of the targe. The soldiers were instructed to thrust with the bayonet at the clansman on their right and not at the man opposed directly to them. If this drill was carried out in battle, the British discipline must have been first class, for the soldier needed to have implicit confidence in his comrade on his left.

On 14 April Cumberland reached Nairn. Leisurely as his advance may seem, he still had the great advantage that his men knew themselves to be following the rebels. There is little except victory itself more calculated to raise the morale of an army than to be following a retreating enemy. Likewise, always to be falling back is one of the most depressing operations in war.

At last, on 16 April, the two armies came face to face on Drumossie Moor, the other name for the battle of Culloden. Cumberland marched from Nairn on that day, and in one last bid for victory Charles ordered a night attack on Cumberland's camp, but it was never delivered owing to misdirection of the Highland columns. The clansmen returned to their original positions on the moor, hungry, tired and dispirited. Cumberland, whatever his failings in the higher branches of generalship, understood how to manage his soldiers. He was popular with them and known to them as 'Billy'. The day before the battle was his birthday and he gave this as his reason for issuing extra food and drink to the troops. When he set out on the march towards the Prince's army, his men were confident of victory. His army had a strength of about 8,000 to 9,000 men; Charles's 4,000 to 5,000. He had eighteen guns well served by regulars of Captain Cunningham's Company, while Charles's fewer guns were poorly served by amateurs and Highlanders who were quite inexpert in their use. Cumberland's cavalry consisted of Cobham's Dragoons (now the 10th Hussars), Lord Mark Kerr's Dragoons (the 11th Hussars) and Kingston's Horse (now disbanded), superior in numbers to the Jacobite cavalry but probably inferior in quality. There were seventeen foot regiments or formations in Cumberland's army, and of these about 1,000 were the Argyll Militia, that is Highlanders. There were in the regular infantry: the Royal Scots, the Royal Scots Fusiliers, the King's Own Scottish Borderers (to give modern names for the second and third of these), and the Royal Inniskilling Fusiliers. Thus the picture often presented by some Scottish writers of Scotland being finally defeated by England at Culloden is quite wrong. Making a not ungenerous computation, between a quarter and a third of the royal troops at Culloden were Scots.[3] In the whole of Scotland the Prince's armed supporters never totalled more than 8,000, of whom 7,000 were Highlanders. Jacobite support in the Lowlands was the minimal part of the Prince's army. Nearly 13,000 Scots enlisted in militia and other auxiliary forces to serve King George. The clans which held aloof were those of Campbell, Mackay, Munro, Macpherson (except for Cluny), Grant and Fraser (until after Prestonpans, and then not wholly); the Macleods, Macleans, Macneils and Macdonalds of the Isles.[4]

Against an army nearly double the size of his own, well trained and equipped with efficient artillery, the Prince had no hope of success. When within some 500 yards of the Jacobites, Cumberland's artillery opened fire. As if they had no other disadvantages, the Highlanders were posted on an open moor where they were exposed to a devastating fire from the royal guns. Among other horrors of eighteenth-century warfare was that of discharge of grape.

> When bags of balls men fired at once
> When they did spread, hard was the chance,
> It hewed them down, aye, score by score,
> As grass does fall before the mower[5]

By contrast, the fire from the Jacobite guns was feeble and ineffective. To make matters worse for the clansmen who stood in close-packed lines, the wind blew in their faces and sleet and mist hid the royal lines from them, except when a flash from the guns showed that death was about to come hurtling among them. It would have been a frightful ordeal for regular troops and it was too much to expect brave men accustomed to hand-to-hand combat to endure such punishment. The chiefs at the head of their clans sent word to the Prince that they could not hold back their men much longer and that they must charge, yet the cannonade by Cumberland's gunners may have lasted half an hour before the Highland charge began. Like most things in the '45, the duration of the gunfire is given variously by different writers, but the cannonade did not cease even when the Highlanders began to charge. Grape was poured into them at ever lessening range.

First into the attack were the Mackintoshes of 'Colonel Anne's' regiment, and the rest were not far behind. Just as Hawley's and Cumberland's order had analysed it, the charge of these wild men from the hills formed itself without any intention into wedges. Little wonder that it had dismayed troops who were trained to fight in continental wars where lines of disciplined infantry faced each other. But now the redcoats were trained and ready. They stood firmly in their ranks, bayonets fixed, until the order was given to make ready, to present and—when the racing clansmen were at not more than thirty yards' distance—to fire. The front rank knelt to fire, while behind it the second rank was firing, and the third rank took a pace to the right and fired while the front rank knelt again to pour in yet another volley.

Very few of the clansmen could survive such a cool, calculated roll of musketry, the forerunner of the famous 'five rounds rapid' of the next century. Some of these heroic men did get up to Barrell's (now King's Own Royal Regiment) and what was left of eight clan regiments broke through, or else Barrell's split by order. The left half of Munro's also received the brunt of the Highlander's charge. Barrell's had stood firm at Falkirk, while Munro's had broken, but now it fought as spiritedly as Barrell's. There are the usual conflicting accounts; on the Jacobite side an assertion that after the Highland attack only two of Barrell's men were able to stand, and from an officer of Munro's a claim that his regiment defeated the rebels almost single-handed, laying 1,600 dead on the spot. In fact, some 500 men are thought to have penetrated Cumberland's line, but he had quickly arranged to bring up supporting troops, apart from his second line. Very few indeed of the Highlanders returned alive from the charge and those who did were wounded. Barrell's regiment had, it appears, split in two by direction and those clansmen who came through the opening were exposed to two fires, and to the very destructive use of the bayonet on the new principle previously mentioned.

The furious attack thus broken was that of the rebels' right wing against Cumberland's left, whereas the Highland left wing merely made some movements towards the royal right and then retired. It appears that the ground was more difficult for a charge on the left of the Highland line. The Macdonalds of Keppoch were posted there, contrary to their usual position on the right wing which they claimed had been their privilege since Bannockburn. They also hung back at first from the charge because of the awkward nature of the ground, which was thought to hide a morass. When Keppoch saw his clansmen hesitating he exclaimed angrily, 'My God, have my children [ie, clan] deserted me?' Keppoch was mortally wounded soon after and a legend has grown up of Macdonalds standing indifferently in the line watching their chief die, and all because their pride was affronted by being placed on the left of the Prince's line. There is enough sadly romantic fact in the end of Jacobitism without the need of such invention. The Macdonalds charged and were met by a withering fire from the Royals and Pulteneys. Unlike their comrades on the left, the Macdonalds did not come on in one maddened onslaught but made three rushes in the hopes of getting the redcoats to advance.

The battle was over. The moor was thick with dead and wounded. Cumberland rode along the ranks, congratulating his brave boys who responded with their caps or hats on the points of their bayonets, and shouts of 'Billy, Billy' and 'Flanders, Flanders'. Having done their work they wanted to return to warfare against civilised opponents.

Neither Cumberland nor his officers could have realised that the tactics they had used against the Highlanders and which had broken their charge would be employed in a hundred battles all over the world when the British army would meet and beat the onslaught of savages. Savages the Highlanders were called by the Lowlanders and, opprobrious though the term was, there could be no question but that the clansmen were wild, undisciplined fighters. Having mastered them, the British troops had learned how to meet Afridis, Zulus, Maoris, American Indians, Ethiopians and Dervishes, all determined warriors. A steady and disciplined fire at close range—'Wait till you see the whites of their eyes!'—and reception of the survivors on the bayonets was to win battle after battle for British troops. In the hundred years from 1815 to 1914, British soldiers fought once in Europe (the Crimean War 1854–6) and once outside Europe against white men (in South Africa 1899–1902), but in conflicts with native races in several continents no army had as much experience as the British. The foundation of its success against this type of adversary can be traced to the victory at Culloden.

So far the events had been honourable for Cumberland and his men, but the aftermath of victory was to see incidents almost as horrible as any in the history of British warfare. The story that the Highlanders had promised no quarter to the royal troops had been industriously put around, and Cumberland, in his turn, showed them no quarter. The killing of Charles Fraser of Inverallochie is attributed to Cumberland but it is thought to be more applicable to Hawley. He ordered James Wolfe, later the conqueror of Quebec, to shoot Fraser and when he refused, offering to resign his commission, a soldier was found to finish off the wounded man. Cumberland was no more squeamish and all over the battlefield the royal troops were encouraged to despatch their wounded enemies.

The Prince, whose courage was undoubted, might have been

wiser to have charged into Cumberland's ranks and been slain. As it was, he suffered his bridle to be taken by an aide-de-camp and to be led from the field. He spent the night after the battle at a house about twenty miles from Culloden. Later, there was much talk, and there has been much writing since, about a fresh gathering of the clans to renew the war, but nothing of the sort occurred and there is hardly an instance of armed resistance from the clansmen as Cumberland's troops searched the Highlands. One might have expected a fierce guerilla warfare from glen to glen, but perhaps Culloden had been too bitter a lesson. Estimates of the number of Jacobite dead vary from about 2,000 to 750. Many of the wounded crawled away to die so that their bodies were not found on the battlefield. They were fortunate in some respects. Those who could not move from the moor lay there for two days, and were for the most part killed when the troops went over the ground. Parties of troops were sent out to search houses near the battlefield. Any rebels found there were generally brought out and shot. In some cases the houses or farm buildings were set on fire with the rebel occupants inside. There were cases of civilians who had been confounded with the Jacobites on the roads near Culloden and were killed along with them by the royal cavalry. Men who had taken no part in the rebellion were quite often shot by the soldiers, and so were some who had been given safe conduct by the authorities. Plundering was regulated by the Duke's orders that articles of value had to be handed in and credit given for them. Every species of armed violence was not only tolerated but encouraged. Wanton destruction was done to the property of rebels, and in the case of large houses and estates, this often took the form of destroying valuable or useful articles, rows of trees, or ornaments in stone. In the case of the poorer clansmen, their humble dwellings were burned down, their cattle driven off and their families forced out into the open.

The author of the '45 endured six months of wandering in the Highlands, during which time he was constantly sought by the British troops and often hemmed round by his enemies. Despite all these dangers, the Prince escaped, guarded as he was by close friends and protected by many humble persons. He took now to wearing the kilt which he had not done before.

As for food and drink, he fared very well though his friends could not get him any bread. At last, in September, he escaped on a French ship from Morlaix, near South Uist. The Prince's year was over.

Many of the leaders, like Lord George Murray and Lochiel, escaped to France after numerous adventures. Cluny remained hidden on his estates for years, and the devotion shown to these fallen great ones by their lowly dependants was the last manifestation of the old half-feudal, half-clan spirit. When Scott made Fergus MacIvor talk of the effects of John Bull's fight in the '45, he was describing the Government's measures to ensure that the Highlanders should never rise again. A new Disarming Act was passed and much more rigorously enforced; the Highland dress was proscribed under very severe penalties, any repetition of the offence of wearing it being punishable by transportation. The old hereditary claims of feudal superiors to military service were abolished. Those chiefs of clans loyal to Government were paid compensation, the total sum being £152,237 15s 4d of which Argyll received £21,000 (Lang, op cit, vol 4, p 522). And when the rebellion was over Argyll and his clansmen, and some of the other Government clans, were given one last chance to carry out a fire and sword policy against their enemies.

At Culloden, the Duke of Cumberland fairly earned the title of 'The Butcher', and within twenty years of that momentous battle Jacobitism was dead in the Highlands, and therefore everywhere else.

11　From Disaster to Triumph

IN 1773, FROM August to November, Dr Samuel Johnson visited the Scottish Highlands, passing through the Great Glen by Loch Ness and so on to the Hebridean islands of Skye, Raasay, Col, Mull, Inchkenneth and Icolmhill. Later he passed by way of Lochlomond and Dumbarton to Glasgow, to Ayrshire and so back to Edinburgh. Throughout the journey he was accompanied by his future biographer, James Boswell. The account of their travels is of particular interest because it gives a picture of the Highlanders in the very difficult period of the generation after Culloden. The Highland chiefs no longer had the power to evict their tenants if they would not follow them in war. The clansmen were now effectually disarmed and their traditional dress was proscribed. But much of the old way of life lingered, and in several places the travellers required an interpreter.

Johnson's hostility to the Scotch is apparent to every reader of the famous *Life*, though it was probably more affectation than reality as his book, *A Journey to the Western Islands of Scotland*, is completely free from prejudices as far as Highlanders are concerned. Indeed, he is pro-Highland in his sympathies. On the subject of their disarmament, he remarks that in their isolated and exposed situation, the clansmen, having been disarmed, are deprived of the means of defending themselves and yet the British Government is not in a position to defend them promptly. Johnson described the state of the Highlanders:

> Their pride has been crushed by the heavy hand of a vindictive conqueror, whose severities have been followed by laws, which, though they cannot be called cruel, have produced much discontent, because they operate upon the surface of life, and make every eye bear witness to subjection. To be compelled to a new dress has always been found painful. Their chiefs being now deprived of their jurisdiction, have

already lost much of their influence and as they gradually degenerate from patriarchal rulers to rapacious landlords, they will divest themselves of the little that remains.

This, as will be seen, was a very true forecast. The disarming after Culloden had been effective and general, as it had not been after 1715. Johnson commented:

> The roads are secure in those places through which, forty years ago, no traveller could pass without a convoy. All trials of right by the sword are forgotten, and the mean are in as little danger from the powerful as in other places.

The problem remained of finding work for the Highlanders. One course adopted by the Government was to utilise the war-like spirit of the clans on foreign fields, and according to the account in Frank Adams's book (p 272), the scheme for forming some half-dozen Highland regiments, on the lines of the Black Watch already formed in 1739, was put forward by Lord President Forbes of Culloden. Sir Robert Walpole, then Premier, liked the idea but as the '45 rising occurred at the time, the Cabinet turned down the scheme. Years later William Pitt, later Earl of Chatham, revived it. As a result, the Highland regiments fought in the Seven Years' War and one of their great triumphs took place at the battle of Quebec in 1759 where the general was the same James Wolfe who had refused to kill the wounded Highlander at Culloden. In his speech in Parliament in 1766 Pitt said:

> I sought for merit wherever it was to be found, it is my boast that I was the first minister who looked for it and found it in the mountains of the north. I called it forth and drew into your service a hardy and intrepid race of men, who when left by your jealousy became a prey to the artifices of your enemies, and had gone nigh to have overturned the state in the war before the last. These men in the last war were brought to combat on your side; they served with fidelity as they fought with valour, and conquered for you in every part of the world. [Quoted in Adams, p 273.]

War alone could not absorb all the surplus population, nor could it take the women as well as the men. Emigration was the alternative and very soon whole sections of the Highland population went out to Canada and the American colonies. The movement was to be powerfully assisted by the means which Dr Johnson foresaw—the Highland Clearances began. If money had become important and rentals were everything, then the chiefs had to get the best possible returns on their lands. Briefly and starkly, the land was cleared of the clansmen,

M

who were evicted from their little crofts and had their homes burnt. Many were taken to the coast where they failed to make a success of the fishing, though some derived a meagre living from gathering kelp for use as a fertiliser during the sixty-odd years the industry lasted. In many cases the Highlanders were put on board ship by force and taken off to Canada or Australia.

The periods of the major clearances were in the years 1782–1820 and between 1840 and 1854. The introduction of a famous breed of sheep, the Great Cheviot, accounted for most of the clearances. Sheep, and later deer for sport in stalking, were preferred to men. In the Victorian era it was possible to disguise the ill-treatment of the poor under pompous platitudes. 'After 1745, there was no further interruption. The interests of civilisation, that is, the interests of knowledge, of liberty, and of wealth, gradually assumed the upper hand, and reduced men like the Highlanders to utter insignificance.' (H. T. Buckle, *History of Civilization*, 1857–61, ch 3, 'Condition of Scotland during the 17th and 18th Centuries'.)

The historian of civilisation might write like this in the full belief that he was right. Buckle's book was published in 1857, and conveniently ignored the fact that at the time of the recently ended Crimean War, it had been impossible to raise recruits for the Highland regiments. The young men were simply not there. 'An island rent-roll, once counted in swordsmen, now depended on the manuring of English fields.' (John Prebble, *The Highland Clearances* (1969 edition), p 249.) Not for long, however. The need for kelp slackened disastrously at the end of the Napoleonic Wars. 'The industry continued in decline for another quarter of a century but long before then the people who had been drawn to the islands to work it were being driven out, and the great seaweed chiefs sank into a bankruptcy from which only the Great Cheviot could rescue them.' (John Prebble, ibidem, p 250.) The strangest feature of the Clearances was that the men made hardly any resistance, astonishing indeed from a race whose ancestors had been so martial. Women, aided by boys, opposed the sheriffs' men, the police, and in some cases the soldiers who were sent to evict them. The eviction of the Rosses of Strathcarron is a disgraceful story of women being knocked down and brutally ill-treated by the police.

The legislation against the Macgregors was repealed in 1774 and the ban on Highland dress lifted in 1782, the year which saw the beginning of the Highland Clearances. Simultaneously with the removal of the clansmen from their native glens, there began the modern movement to romanticise the Gael, a movement which within a very short time had made Highlander synonymous with Scotsman, and the so-called 'garb of old Gaul' the usual style of dress in which all manner of Scots were depicted. The Highlanders having been got rid of and sent off by shiploads to the colonies, the Highland idea was taken up with enthusiasm but without much thought. Tartans which can clearly be seen as quite different from those used by clans before the '45 began to be woven and adopted by the clans. The well-known firm of Wilsons, situated patriotically at Bannockburn, began their business of tartan production which was to last for nearly 200 years.

King George IV's visit to Edinburgh in 1822 saw the first identification of Highland dress as that of the whole nation, and most present-day tartans go back to that period. With regard to this movement, a Highland Scot who could not be accused of lack of patriotism has written:

> In this way, the dress of the so-called 'half-naked savages' has become by tacit consent the national costume of Scotland. The tartan has become the distinguishing uniform of the Scottish regiments—Lowland as well as Highland. The bagpipe has become the national musical instrument and the Celt who was supposed by partisan historians to have been vanquished at Harlaw and Culloden, has impressed his own characteristics on the Scottish nationality. It has been claimed that the dress is a Lowland as well as a Highland costume. We cannot find a shadow of proof for such a claim in the writings of the old historians either native or foreign. [J. G. Mackay, *The Romantic Story of the Highland Garb and the Tartan*, 1924, p 30.] Ibidem: So-called Lowland Family Tartans have made their appearance within modern times [p 31].

Not all Scots realise the enormous influence that Sir Walter Scott had on their country's fortune, an influence acknowledged by one of the most recent writers on Highland dress: 'It took a Sir Walter Scott to bring the garb back to some form of popularity. Under his direction the Scottish nobility resumed this ancient dress on the occasion of the visit of George IV to Edinburgh. His Majesty appeared resplendent in kilt and plaid and Sir Walter likewise.' (R. M. D. Grange, *A Short History of the Scottish Dress*, 1966, p 98.)

Yet Scott himself was still half dubious about the ascription of tartan-wearing to Lowlanders. In a letter to Sir Thomas Dick Lauder, dated 5 June 1829, he wrote:

> The general proposition that the Lowlanders ever wore plaids is difficult to swallow. They were of twenty different races and almost all distinctly different from the Scots Irish, who are the proper Scots, from which the Royal Family are descended. For instance, there is scarce a great family in the Lowlands of Scotland that is not to be traced to the Normans. . . . Is it natural to think that holding the Scots in the contempt in which they did, they would have adopted their dress? If you will look at Bruce's speech to David I as the historian Aelred tells the story, you will see he talks of the Scots as a British officer would do of Cherokees. [Quoted in *History of Highland Dress*, J. Telfer Dunbar, 1962, p 118.]

Further in a letter dated 19 November 1829 to Sir Thomas Lauder, Scott wrote:

> To suppose Lowlanders to be Highlanders we must suppose that they spoke the Gaelic and held the system of clanship. Without this there could be no occasion for wearing clan tartans. Now every law or regulation concerning clanship is limited to the Highlands and to the Borders. . . . The idea of distinguishing the clans by their tartans is but a fashion of modern date in the Highlands themselves. [Ibidem, p 124.]

In 1842 the mysterious Sobieski Stuart brothers published their massive *Vestiarium Scoticum*. It contained a list of Highland clans followed by the Lowland houses and border clans. Their other work, *The Costume of the Clans* (1845) weighed 22lb. Anent the brothers' work, Miss Macdonald of Glengarry wrote in *Blackwood's Magazine* (April 1895) that she believed them to have invented both Royal Stuart and Stuart hunting tartan. In this connection, although Prince Charles Edward did not himself assume the kilt or plaid until he was a fugitive after Culloden, he is now usually portrayed in either Highland dress or the alleged Stuart tartan, a costume to which his contemporary portraits bear little resemblance. James Logan, who published in 1833 *The Scottish Gael or Celtic Manners, etc*, was in correspondence with Messrs Wilson. He asked for lists of tartans and the firm answered that some of his were 'fancy', 'defective' or 'never seen before'. We can almost see the clan tartans in the making.

For the great occasion of his Edinburgh visit in 1822, the first paid by a reigning sovereign since Charles II, King George IV was dressed by the Laird of Garth in full Highland garb, the same brilliant so-called Stuart tartan, in which certainly no Stuart, except perhaps Prince Charles, might have presented himself in the salons of Holyrood (and then not in a kilt). Garth pronounced George when thus attired 'a very pretty man'. This incident is quoted by Albert McKie in *Scottish Pageantry*, 1967, p 163, from Lockhart's *Life of Scott*. Unfortunately, one of the English magnates who accompanied the King to Holyrood also appeared in the same Stuart tartan. This was Sir William Curtis, from the Guildhall, London, and his appearance prompted a satirical verse by Byron, saying that the chiefs of every Highland clan 'hail their brother Vich Ian Alderman', the allusion being to the fictitious Highland chief in *Waverley*. As Sir William's figure was corpulent, it can be imagined what scope he gave to the cartoonists.

The despised 'savages', however, had triumphed vicariously. Highland dress, either as day or evening wear, is one of the most becoming of all male costumes. With the King and the Scots nobles adopting it, and with Sir Walter Scott as the brilliant manager of the exhibition, the garb caught on, and along with it went a new sentimental appreciation of the Highlanders.

Hound them, kill them, and if that is not enough to finish the clans, drive them out of their poor shelters and force them on board ships, bound like convicts for the penal settlements.

Yet today all over the world there are clan associations and clan gatherings. In the Highlands, several descendants of long lines of chiefs have made their way back to their homeland, and succeeded in purchasing the old castle and a few acres. It says much for the loyal and basically gentle nature of the Highlander that despite the sufferings of clansmen at the hands of their chiefs when they were driven out in favour of sheep rearing, they handed on no legacy of bitterness to their children. Wherever the Highlander goes, wherever he lives, his heart is Highland. When one stands on the great stone on Drumossie Moor and looks across the bleak landscape, with its graves of the clansmen, perhaps one may even dare to think that these men did not die in vain. *O exoriare aliquis* must have been the wish of many an exiled heart, but vengeance when it came was really reconciliation. Scotland identified herself with the Gael and took his traditions for her own.

Notes and References

CHAPTER ONE

(pages 9 to 16)

1   The figure of 31,930 as an estimate of the number of fighting men in the Highlands was given by a contemporary, on the Government side, the Rt Hon Duncan Forbes of Culloden, Lord President of the Court of Session.

2   On the conduct of the English militia, see the scathing comments by Corelli Barnett, *History of the British Army*, 1970.

3   The quotation from Tacitus is taken from his *Agricola* under the year 84.

4   Regarding the treatment of the American Indians, see *A Pictorial History of the American Indian*, Oliver La Farge, 1956, and most modern histories of America.

5   The Clan map of Scotland in Frank Adams' *The Clans, Septs and Regiments of the Scottish Highlands*, 1908, shows the country below the Highland line as void of clan names. In later works, eg, Robert Bain's *Clans and Tartans of Scotland*, 1938–60, clan names are shown all over Scotland.

CHAPTER TWO

(pages 18 to 26)

1   The writings of Tacitus, who wrote around the end of the first
century AD, include the *Histories*, the *Annals*, a life of *Agricola* and
the *Germania*, an account of Germany. The details in the text about
Agricola's campaigns are taken from the Life.

2   Hilaire Belloc in *A History of England*, vol 1 (1925), p 60, wrote
'The Highlands remained unRomanised; which omission has been
felt in history with an effect only less than the refusal to Romanise
Ireland. For it was on account of the Roman failure to subdue the
Highlands, that, when Roman Britain continued as the Britain of
the Dark Ages from St Augustine to Edward the Confessor, Scotland, under Highland kings, developed into an independent state.'
    Edward Gibbon held less exalted views of the matter. He men-
tioned the estimate given by Agricola in the Life that one legion
and some auxiliaries would have been sufficient to conquer Ireland,
and added one of his amusing notes: 'The Irish writers, jealous of
their national honour, are extremely provoked on this occasion,
both with Tacitus and with Agricola.' (*Decline and Fall*, ch 1.)
    It was also Gibbon,who, in the same chapter, commenting on the
Roman refusal to conquer Scotland north of the Antonine Wall,
remarked: 'The masters of the fairest and most wealthy climates of
the globe turned with contempt from gloomy hills assailed by the
winter tempest, from lakes concealed in a blue mist, and from cold
and lonely heaths, over which the deer of the forest were chased
by a troop of naked barbarians.' For full details of the Papal permit
to Henry II, see *Irish Historical Documents* (1968): E. Curtis and
R. B. McDowell.

3   *Mons Graupius.* Tacitus, *Agricola*, c 29. *Ad montem Graupium.* In
some Latin texts edited by modern authors the name has been boldly
put as Grampium. On this, Professor J. B. Bury remarked, 'It has
nothing to do with the Grampians.' (*History of the Roman Empire*,
1893, p 401.)

4 Severus and his invasion of the north of Scotland. See the treatment in rounded, classical turns of phrase in Gibbon, *Decline and Fall*, ch 6, p 15. The tribes broke through into southern Britain. Theodosius reduced the barbarians in Britain in his campaigns in 368 and 369. From the accounts given, even the walled city of London was thought to be in danger from the barbarian marauders (Gibbon, ch 25).

5 Procopius. 'While he lived far away in the eastern empire and was prepared to believe some very queer things about Britain, he probably derived his information from Angles who are known to have accompanied a Frankish embassy to Constantinople in his day.' (*Roman Britain and the English Settlements*, R. G. Collingwood and J. N. L. Myres, 1937, p 337.) Some of the stories in Procopius are tall indeed. See Gibbon, ch 38.

6 Reliefs of Pictish warriors. See, for example of the oriental style, the illustration in Sir Fitzroy Maclean's *Concise History of Scotland*, 1970, p 14.

7 Full details of the Stone of Destiny are given in Appendix 2 of Sir Thomas Innes of Learney's edition of Frank Adams' book *The Clans, Septs and Regiments of the Scottish Highlands*, 1960.

8 The references to Scottish history can be supplemented from many books. Andrew Lang's four-volume *History of Scotland* is always good reading and gives a great deal of detail. Much more condensed but a very good summary is Rosalind Mitchison's *History of Scotland*. The work by Sir Fitzroy Maclean mentioned above gives a good potted survey and is copiously illustrated.

CHAPTER THREE

(pages 27 to 34)

1 Audrey Cunningham, *The Loyal Clans*, 1932, p 44.

2 Sir Thomas Innes' edition of Frank Adams' book, *The Clans, Septs and Regiments of the Scottish Highlands*, 1960, p 232.

3 See *Burke's Landed Gentry of Ireland*, 1958, where many of the pedigrees mentioned are given; also Professor David Greene's article on the Celtic Genealogies in the same work.

4 For very detailed accounts of the personalities of the Norman era see Freeman's *Norman Conquest*.

5 On the subject of Scottish surnames, the best guide is *The Surnames of Scotland, Their Origin, Meaning and History*, George F. Black, New York Public Library, 1962. The passage quoted is from p 13.

6 See the article on this family in *Burke's Landed Gentry*, editions 1937–52.

7 The quotation is from the article 'Drummond, Earls of Perth' in *Burke's Peerage*.

8 See the most interesting account of Edgar's coronation rites in *A History of the English Coronation*, Professor P. E. Schramm (Oxford 1937).

9 Full discussion of the feudal supremacy of the English monarchy over the Scottish king will be found in Andrew Lang's *History of Scotland*, vol 1, pp 44–6.

10 The quotation is from Lang, op cit, p 98.

11 For early Berkeley history, see under that name, *Burke's Peerage*.

CHAPTER FOUR

(pages 36 to 51)

1 From Sir Thomas Innes's edition of Frank Adams' book, op cit, p 232.

2 From Lang, *History of Scotland*, vol 1, p 123.

3 From Lang, op cit, vol 1, p 263. The title 'Lord James' is a curious expression. The early Douglas lords derived their surname from Douglas (a Gaelic name meaning 'dark water') in Lanarkshire. They were the feudal lords of Douglas and soon took their surname from their lands as did most of their class. The expressions 'Lord James of Douglas' and the 'Good Sir James of Douglas', as purporting to be used in the fourteenth century, are hardly to be described as anachronisms, but are curious misnomers.

4 The lines of ballad are from Sir Walter Scott's *The Antiquary*, ch 40.

5 The quotation is from Audrey Cunningham, *The Loyal Clans*, p 58.

6 Wolf of Badenoch: see Lang, op cit, vol 1, p 284.

7 Lang, op cit, p 284.

8 From Sir Walter Scott's Introduction to *The Fair Maid of Perth*. The reference to Lang is to his vol 1, p 285.

9 See Eyre Todd, *The Highland Clans of Scotland; Their History and Traditions*, 1923, under Clan Cameron, vol 1, p 20.

10 From Sir Walter Scott, *The Fair Maid of Perth*, end of ch 34.

11 Details of the headship of Clan Chattan can be seen under the articles in *Burke's Landed Gentry*, ie, Mackintosh and Macpherson; also in Sir Thomas Innes's edition of Adams' book, under Mackintosh, pp 249–51.

12 Details of the three Acts are taken from W. F. Skene's work, *Celtic Scotland: A History of Ancient Alban*, 1876, vol 3, 'The Land and People', p 327, *et seq*. In the same volume there is a very detailed account of the Highland Line. Another reference is to an Act of

1594 in which the Highland areas are described in detail. This reference comes from *A Short History of the Scottish Dress*, R. M. D. Grange, 1966. The author states (p 20) 'It has never been decided to what extent of the country the name "Highland" applied. The above mentions the Earl of Huntly as being a Highlander and in 1385, when Robert II was at Stirling, he was considered to be in the Highlands. That the term covered a far greater area than today is certain.' Sometimes (eg, in Sir Walter Scott's *Guy Mannering*) the term 'Highland' is applied to the hilly country of the Borders.

CHAPTER FIVE

(pages 53 to 66)

1 On the subject of Highland dress the student should consult the following works, to which reference is made in the text: *Old Irish and Highland Dress and that of the Isle of Man*, H. F. McClintock, 2nd and enlarged edition, 1950, published by Dundalgan Press (W. Tempest) Ltd, Dundalk. It is very well illustrated and includes chapters on pre-Norman dress as described in early Irish literature by the Rev Professor F. Shaw, sj, ma, and on 'Early Tartans' by J. Telfer Dunbar, fsa scot. The book is bound with *Old Highland Dress and Tartans*, H. F. McClintock, with a chapter on Early Tartans by J. Telfer Dunbar (1949). The last-named brought out a *History of Highland Dress*, 1962: a definitive study of the history of Scottish costume and tartan, both civil and military, including weapons: with an appendix on 'Early Scottish Dyes' by Annette Kok.

As regards the arrangement of the tartans, the best work is D. C. Stewart's *The Setts of the Scottish Tartans*, 1950. J. G. MacKay, mbe, jp, Portree, wrote *The Romantic Story of the Highland Garb and the Tartan*, 1924, published by Eneas Mackay, Stirling, in an edition limited to 575 copies. This has an appendix by Lt-Colonel Norman Macleod, cmg, dso, dealing with the kilt in the 1914–18 war. See also *A Short History of the Scottish Dress*, R. M. D. Grange, 1966, with a foreword by Sir Iain Moncreiffe of that Ilk.

A large number of books give tartan patterns, while older and larger works contain much information about various aspects of Highland dress and culture. *A History of the Scottish Highland Clans and Regiments* contains an account of the Gaelic Language, Literature and Music by the Rev Thomas Maclauchlan, lld, fsa scot, and an essay on Highland Scenery by the late Professor John Wilson. The editor is John S. Keltie, fsa scot, and the regimental portion has been brought up to the present time from official sources by William Melven, ma Glasgow. There is no date, but the work was published in five volumes by William Mackenzie of 69 Ludgate Hill, London.

A very excellent and well-balanced book is *Scottish Pageantry*, Albert Mackie, 1967 (Hutchinson). In this work the Highland dress necessarily figures but there is much else besides of great value. The author remarks *inter alia* (p 17) 'The Scots of the Borders are no more Scots in the racial sense of Dalriadic Gaels than the men of the Boston Tea Party were Red Indians.' Again (p 25) 'The Lowland soldiers also wear tartan trews. This is significant of the fact that tartan, once regarded as exclusively Highland, has become accepted as the national garb. Two hundred years after the kilt and its accessories were banned to put an end to Highland rebellion the tartan is saluted as the worthy wear of any patriotic Scot, even if some of us still hesitate through Lowland bashfulness to wear it.'

2 Considerable ingenuity was shown by the old Highlanders in obtaining dyes from plants and lichens with which to get the numerous colours mentioned in connection with their garments. Fir club moss was used in place of alum. Blackberries gave a purple dye, and oak galls produced black. Annette Kok, in the essay mentioned above, describes the difficulty of obtaining blue and red from the native British dye-plants. 'It seems that imported foreign dye-stuffs must have been used to a certain extent in the Highlands from quite an early date, especially for blue [op cit, p 226].' Indigo was sent from Holland to St Kilda from 1700. This gave the Highland dyer a variety of blues and, by using it on yellow and crimson grounds, a wide range of greens and purples was made possible. It may be that difficulties in making some colours retarded the development of tartans in older times.

3 Albert Mackie in *Scottish Pageantry*.

4 Quotation from Stuart, *et seq*, from J. Telfer Dunbar, op cit, p 70.

5 The verse quoted as expressing Sir John Sinclair's view is given in J. Telfer Dunbar, op cit, p 185.

6 The quotation is from *European and American Arms*, Claud Blair, 1962, p 28 and illustration Xf.

CHAPTER SIX

(pages 74 to 89)

In general, the sources for this chapter are as in other chapters, ie, *History of the Scottish Highlands* (with more detail than any other work), edited by John S. Keltie, 5 vols; Andrew Lang's *History of Scotland*, 4 vols. Three modern presentations of Scottish history (but in far less detail) are given in: *The Royal House of Scotland*, Eric Linklater; *A Concise History of Scotland*, Sir Fitzroy Maclean; and *A History of Scotland*, Rosalind Mitchison, 1 volume each.

1   Older writers considered James IV to have had a good knowledge of the language but a more modern writer thinks he had only a smattering. Eric Linklater, op cit, p 53.

2   Audrey Cunningham, *The Loyal Clans*, ch 5, 'The Royal Lieutenants'.

3   Sir Robert Gordon (1580–1656), the historian of the Sutherlands, Earls of Sutherland, described in the DNB as fourth son of Alexander, 11th or 12th Earl of Sutherland, but in current *Burke's Peerage* as a younger son of Alexander, 12th Earl of Sutherland. Sir Robert was a gentleman of the privy chamber to James I and Charles I. He married Louisa, daughter and heiress of John Gordon of Glenluce, was created a baronet of Nova Scotia, 1625, and was the author of *The Genealogical History of the Earldom of Sutherland*, edited in 1813 by Henry Weber.

4   Audrey Cunningham, op cit, ch 6, 'The Clan Gregor'.

5   See Sir Thomas Innes of Learney's edition of Frank Adams' *Clans, Septs and Regiments of the Scottish Highlands*, p 247.

GENERAL NOTE: *Manners in the Highlands in the fifteenth to seventeenth centuries:*
It may be thought that historians of the Highlands have been selective at times in their treatment and have tended to give prominence

to lurid incidents. As a corrective to what might be considered a one-sided view, it is instructive to read some of the family histories of the Highland chiefs in the volumes of *Burke's Peerage* or *Burke's Landed Gentry*, all of which were approved by the families concerned. In the latter volume, looking through articles under the letter 'M', the following true stories are told.

Under MacDonald of Balranald, the tale is given of the chief of Banranald, Donald, by whom that property and much of North Uist was held, about 1470. By his natural brother, Gillespie Dubh, he was induced to enter a jumping contest in his hall. Gillespie arranged for an accomplice to be concealed in a gallery and to drop a noose over the chief's head as he jumped. Gillespie then ran a red hot spit through Donald's body. He also killed his eldest natural brother. Donald's son killed Gillespie while they were out hunting.

Under Mackintosh of Mackintosh, there are some colourful details. In 1442 the Comyns invited the chief and his clansmen, with whom they had been at war, to a feast of reconciliation. A Comyn who was in love with a Mackintosh girl told her that when a boar's head was brought into the feast this would be the signal for the Comyns to slaughter the Mackintoshes. Instead, being fore-warned, the Mackintoshes fell on the Comyns, massacred them and regained possession of the Castle of Rait. In 1515, William Mackin-tosh, 13th Chief of Mackintosh and 14th of Clan Chattan, was mur-dered in his bed by John, his second cousin. William's brother, Lachlan, succeeded as 14th Chief and had his brother's thirteen assassins hunted down and beheaded. Hector, natural son of the 12th Chief and Captain of the clan during the chief's minority, was murdered by a priest in 1532. The blood feud between the Mackin-toshes and the Camerons lasted for 300 years. It was finally com-posed in 1665.

Under Macleod of Macleod: Thomas Macleod, 11th Chief, though a minor, was murdered at Dunvegan about 1557, together with his uncle Duncan, captain of the clan, by another uncle, Ian Dubh, who made himself chief but was driven out and murdered in Ireland.

Under Macneil of Barra: the 35th Chief of Clan Niall and 15th of Barra must have been eminent among his contemporaries for he was called 'The Turbulent'. He lived under James VI. He was constantly put to the horn but managed to pass on his chiefship to his son, who was also frequently the subject of proceedings by the Privy Council.

Frazer, or Fraser, under Lovat, B. in *Burke's Peerage*: Simon Fraser,

11th Lord Lovat, had an extraordinary career which closed when he was beheaded on Tower Hill in 1747. His specialities were elopement with, or forcible possession of, the persons of heiresses and a dabbling in politics in which he espoused both sides, Hanoverian and Jacobite, until at last he was caught out for participating in the '45.

The Colquhouns (baronets) have been mentioned as having suffered severely at the hands of the Macgregors, but they were not without breaches of law in their family. Sir Humphrey Colquhoun of Luss was murdered in his castle of Bannachra in 1592 as part of the feud with the Macgregors. His son Alexander was the loser in the hard battle of Glenfruin in 1603. His grandson, Sir John Colquhoun, created a baronet of Nova Scotia, had a criminal case raised against him because he had abducted his sister-in-law, Lady Katharine Graham. For this offence he was not only outlawed but excommunicated as well, for in 1632 the Kirk had become very powerful in Scotland. Sir John's estates were also confiscated but his brother got them back and conveyed them to Sir John's eldest son.

The family histories in these two reference works abound in instances of letters of fire and sword, of executions of chiefs, and forfeiture of estates. Yet, strangely enough, in the majority of cases the wrongdoer escaped punishment and often died peacefully in his bed despite all the threats of Government against him.

N

CHAPTER SEVEN

(pages 97 to 111)

1 The Mackintoshes had been trying for centuries to dislodge the Macdonalds of Keppoch from their lands. In 1684 the Mackintosh chief asked for troops to help him. Nothing was done until 1688 when Mackintosh was given authority to attack the Keppoch men with his own clansmen and allies, plus a company of regular troops under Mackenzie of Suddie. In the ensuing battle the Macdonalds won, but the officer commanding the royal troops was killed. The Government's prestige was now involved and a further force of soldiers was sent to lay waste the Keppoch land and to destroy every man, woman and child of the Macdonalds of that branch. (Cunningham, op cit, p 34.)

2 Calvin's Catechism was translated into Gaelic by John Carswell and published in Edinburgh in 1631. See illustration in Sir Fitzroy Maclean's *Concise History of Scotland*, p 106.

3 There is a good romantic description of Montrose's escape in Scott's *Legend of Montrose*.

4 There were garrisons in the five great forts at Leith, Ayr, Perth, Inverness and Inverlochy (near the present Fort William).

5 Andrew Lang gives some specimens of Cameron's prophecies, which were very wild. Lang, op cit, vol 3, p 357.

6 The Duke of Lauderdale possessed many of the characteristics and qualities which would be ascribed in fictitious narratives to some unscrupulous lord, though much of his manipulation of the Scots law in his own interest did not become known until long after his death. With his countenance and support, the Earl of Argyll was able to recover the position of his family. Conversely, a family opposed to the Duke's, or one which had incurred his enmity, was likely to be depressed and ruined. The ancient and honourable house of the Scrymgeours came within this unfortunate category. The head of this family had received the Viscounty of Dudhope, and later the Earldom of Dundee. The 1st Earl had fought for Charles I and

Charles II, and been present at Worcester. When he died without issue in 1668, he should have been succeeded in his title and estates by his kinsman, John Scrymgeour. 'By the interest of the Duke of Lauderdale with Charles II he was deprived of his right to succeed to the estates of Dudhope, and to the Viscounty and earldom.' The estates were never recovered by the family. The titles were regained by the present holder in 1952 and 1953. A melodramatic feature of this case was the fact that the original patent of nobility was destroyed by Lauderdale to prevent the heirs from knowing the nature of the descent. A full account is given in 'Proceedings before the Committee for Privileges and Judgment in Dudhope Peerage and Earldom of Dundee, 1952 & 1953', (HMSO).

CHAPTER EIGHT

(pages 114 to 126)

1 'Sirs, I here present unto you King George, your undoubted King, etc, etc'—from Coronation Service (1937).

2 James VI's ideal of kingship is given in his *Basilikon Doron*, quoted by Cunningham, op cit, p 371.

3 Keltie, *The Scottish Highlands*. vol 2, p 367. The second quotation is from Lord Macaulay's *History of England*, Everyman edition, vol 2, p 652.

4 The bayonet took its name from a special type of dagger made in Bayonne. Not later than the second quarter of the seventeenth century, the term was applied to a dagger or short sword which was designed to be attached to the muzzle of a gun. The earliest evidence for the military use of the bayonet was in France in 1642. It was not until the third decade of the eighteenth century that the socket bayonet was introduced. Before that the plug bayonet was in use, but it had the serious disadvantage that while it was in position the gun could not be fired. Claude Blair, *European and American Arms*, 1962, p 13. The bayonet superseded the pike.

5 *From Memoirs of Dundee*, quoted in Keltie, op cit, vol 2, p 376.

6 In the Book of Common Order there was a prayer of thanksgiving in which it was said *inter alia* 'Thou of Thine especial Goodness didst move the hearts of our neighbours [of whom we had deserved no such favour] to take upon them the common burden with us and for our deliverance not only to spend the lives of many but also to hazard the estate and tranquillity of their realm and commonwealth.' The whole prayer as given by Cunningham, op cit, p 237, is of great interest.

7 This Gaelic phrase is mentioned in John Prebble's book, *Glencoe*, 1967, p 11.

8 Keltie, op cit, vol 12, p 395.

9 There are many accounts of the massacres but the best and most detailed is that by John Prebble in *Glencoe*, the result of thorough research into every aspect of the matter.

CHAPTER NINE

(pages 130 to 140)

1 See *English Historical Documents,* vol 8, p 677.

2 See *EHD,* vol 8, p 129, *et seq.*

3 The Electress Sophia died 8 June 1714, Queen Anne on 1 August 1714. Sophia was nearly 84.

4 The Scots Parliament passed an Act agreeing to the articles of union on 16 January 1707. Articles of union had been agreed by the commissioners of both countries on 22 July 1706. The Act of Union, with its twenty-five articles, was due to take effect on 1 May 1707. See *EHD,* vol 8, op cit, p 680.

5 This is the incident behind the intrigues in Scott's story, *The Black Dwarf.*

6 The Duke of Argyll's titles take up twelve lines in *Burke's Peerage* and are usually reckoned as nineteen in all.

7 The Treaty of Utrecht ended the War of the Spanish Succession in 1713.

8 Numbers of men in a Highland army varied over a period of weeks or months as the clansmen, not being regular troops, could not be held to a term of engagement and always tended to go home unless action appeared imminent.

9 For example:

> 'There is some say that we wan,
> And some say that they wan,
> And some say that nan wan at a' man,
> But one thing I'm sure
> That at Sheriffmuir
> A battle there was that I saw, man.
> And we ran, and they ran,
> And they ran, and we ran,
> And we ran, and they ran awa', man!'

These are some of the words of an old song, 'The Battle of Sheriffmuir', quoted in Cunningham, op cit, p 449; they come from Hogg's *Jacobite Relics*.

10   Rob Roy was in command of the Macgregors, he being the chief's uncle. The song mentioned in note 9 also commemorates his inactivity:

> 'Rob Roy there stood watch on a hill, for to catch
> The booty, for ought that I saw, man,
> For he ne'er advanced from the place he was stanc'd,
> Till no more was to do there, at a' man.'

This verse is quoted in Keltie, op cit, vol 2, p 465.

11   This letter was never sent. See the detailed account in *The Jacobite Rising of 1715* by John Baynes (1970), p 179. This work, which I did not see until after the present book was completed, is a very valuable study of the '15. L.G.P.

CHAPTER TEN

(pages 148 to 163)

1 For a full treatment of this see *The Princes of Wales*, L. G. Pine; *The Four Georges*, William Thackeray, and *The Impeachment of the House of Brunswick*, Charles Bradlaugh.

2 Hawley's Order Book. Quoted in Tomasson's and Buist's *Battles of the '45*, p 105. In J. Telfer Dunbar's *History of Highland Dress*, p 191, quoted as from the Duke of Cumberland's Orderly Book.

3 See *Battles of the '45*, , K. Tomasson and Francis Buist, p 205. After mentioning the Scots regiments among the royal troops at Culloden, the authors add: 'It is frequently assumed that the atrocities perpetrated after the action were carried out at the instigation of English officers, whereas three of the worst offenders—Major Lockhart, Captain Scott and the naval officer, Fergussone—were Lowland Scots.'

4 Clans which held aloof. The names given in the text are taken from the notes by Dr George S. Pryde, 'Scottish Support for the '45' in *Common Errors in Scottish History*, Historical Association, 1956.

5 By Dougal Graham, quoted in Lang, op cit, vol 4, p 512. On the subject of Culloden, the best up-to-date account is in the study by John Prebble, *Culloden*, 1961.

Index